THE NEW EGO THEORY: EVOLVING CONSCIOUSNESS THROUGH THE DIVINE OPERATING SYSTEM

A PRACTICAL FRAMEWORK FOR REPROGRAMMING REALITY AND REALIZING SOUL POTENTIAL

TIA MARIE

HOUSE OF INDIGO

Copyright ©2024 by Tia Maria

All rights reserved.

No portion of this book may be reproduced in any form without written permission from the publisher or author, except as permitted by U.S. copyright law.

The content of this book is for informational purposes only and is not intended to diagnose, treat, cure, or prevent any condition or disease. You understand that this book is not intended as a substitute for consultation with a licensed practitioner. Please consult with your own physician or healthcare specialist regarding the suggestions and recommendations made in this book. The use of this book implies your acceptance of this disclaimer.

PUBLISHER'S NOTE: HOUSE OF INDIGO

Working with Tia Marie on *The New Ego Theory* has been a true alignment of vision and purpose. At House of Indigo, we believe in the transformative power of conscious collaboration, and partnering with Tia to shape and bring forth her profound work has been an inspiring journey. Tia's dedication to evolving consciousness through practical frameworks and deep wisdom shines in every chapter, and our role has been to support that message in its purest form.

House of Indigo is a multi-media publishing company dedicated to uplifting spiritual leaders and visionaries who are paving the way to new levels of personal transformation. From books to every kind of printed tool that helps unlock potential, we provide platforms to empower voices without dilution or constraint. We're committed to honoring the integrity of our clients' work, allowing their unique perspectives to resonate and inspire on a global scale.

In creating this book, Tia worked closely with Jessica, founder of House of Indigo, to distill her insights while we managed the publishing process, allowing her to focus fully on the heart of her message. At House of Indigo, we understand that each book is more than content—it's a shared journey, one where author and publisher work side by side to ensure the finished work reflects the highest vision and energy.

House of Indigo—Publishing Tools for Transformation, Empowering True Voices.

INTRODUCTION

If there'd been a shortcut to this so-called "spiritual awakening," I would've dove in headfirst, taken the plunge, and swam straight through the depths of myself. But shortcuts don't often exist in real transformation, and neither do abridged versions of becoming whole. I grew up in a fundamentalist Christian home, obedient, well-behaved, and genuinely alive. But even from my youngest memories, I sensed something was off. Why was I always praying, pleading for some salvation that seemed to drift further away each time? The sermons felt rehearsed, the preachers' voices veiled, hypnotic, like a script everyone pretended to believe in. I could sense the cracks and the contradictions —could see right through the dogma to the humanity beneath, and I wasn't impressed.

As a teenager, I turned away from anything labeled "spiritual" or "religious." I threw myself into my career, and twenty years later, at 35, I found myself crushed by the life I'd built. It was misery in high definition. The hustle had stolen my time, and toxic relationships had left bruises on my spirit. Alone, exhausted, desperate, I prayed—not to a man-made concept of god I no longer believed in, but to the divine, to life, to anything that might still listen. I'd achieved everything I set out to achieve, but in the end, I felt empty, trapped in a shell of a life I didn't want.

Then came the awakening.

Awakenings don't follow logic. They rip you from the comfort of whatever life you've cobbled together and make you see with brutal clarity. The direction they pull you in is unnerving, defying every norm you thought you knew. And when you open your eyes, it's like seeing through layers of fog, while every identity you've clung to crumbles in your hands. But if you're willing, if you're relentless enough to keep going, that chaos starts giving way to clarity. A new way of knowing yourself takes root, and with it, a whole new way of creating.

I didn't write this book because I wanted to. I wrote it because I *had* to. It's been living within me, gathering shape and voice, pulling me toward a mission I couldn't ignore. This is *The New Ego Theory: Evolving Consciousness Through the Divine Operating System*—a living methodology for upgrading the very architecture of the mind. These structures and insights are a way forward, a map back home to yourself. They're not about reciting lofty ideas or wearing spiritual practices like a costume; they're about embodying them, breathing them into the marrow of your life until they're inseparable from you.

You're holding a blueprint for something that goes beyond personal growth—it's a reprogramming of the ego itself, an invitation to see your mental landscape as an operating system. Most approaches to "ego" in self-help, collective narratives, and even psychology, have become outdated. They're relics of a time when the mind was viewed as a problem to be managed rather than a tool for shaping reality. But what if the ego isn't a liability? What if it's the essential architecture of your operating system—a system that, once upgraded, could process vast amounts of information and craft your life with a precision born from higher intelligence?

This book explores that vision. It's a call to see the mind as a dynamic interface, with ego as the core operating system that drives every choice and perception. Through this new paradigm, we'll learn to upgrade the ego, to process big data through a deeply intuitive lens, and to craft new mental landscapes rooted in the intelligence that can only emerge when we understand the mechanics of our minds—neurodivergent perspectives included.

There's a whisper here, a calling that feels like standing on the edge of a vast, unexplored land. In the distance, there's something—a glimmer of lights, hazy architecture, the curve of water or a grove of green. An oasis? Maybe. But the urge to walk toward it is primal, instinctual. It's a journey back to something that's been waiting, buried deep. This landscape isn't foreign; it's ancient and familiar, and it's time to return.

This book, *The New Ego Theory*, is your guide to navigating the shift from living as a human trying to touch the soul, to living as a soul fully expressing through the human body. It's a walk across the bridge from where you are to where you were always meant to be. And if you think that sounds strange or pointless, I'll tell you: within this one pinpoint of awareness lies an entire universe of untapped potential.

Let's walk.

DEDICATION

This book is for those who've felt the cracks, the moments when reality as you knew it fell apart, leaving you wondering if it was ever real. It's for the ones who dared to look deeper, even when it hurt, even when the world told you to stop.

To the ones who've been pulled into the storm of awakening, questioning every piece of life you've built, only to find that on the other side of destruction lies creation.

This is your guide, your map, your permission slip to evolve—not by rejecting the ego, but by upgrading it. Because in this journey, the ego isn't the enemy; it's the vehicle that will carry you into your soul's deepest expression.

THE SPIRITUAL DIVERGENT

Welcome to the spaces within you—the ones you've been chasing, the places that haunt your waking hours and light up your nights.

Feel the energy stirring in your bones, thrumming in your cells, a pulse of conscious evolution demanding your attention.

You're here to break free. To diverge from everything that reeks of ordinary, chained, dead, and false.

There's a fire inside you, an untamed force clawing to shatter the cages they handed you at birth.

You've never needed permission.

You've never answered to rules.

You've looked for mirrors but found none that speak your language—none except the one carved into the depths of your own knowing.

You are a universe.

A student.

A seeker of something that can't be contained by words or boundaries.

You're a keeper of patterns, a divine mathematician, an architect of the unseen, a creator who shapes the very fabric of possibility.

You're a genius at your core, an alchemist of reality who won't stop until you feel this wild, raw power settle into its rightful place within you.

This is home, this pulse, this primal memory you carry of a world without walls—a frontier you recognize because you came from it.

But what is it?

PART I

THE NEW EGO THEORY

The New Ego Theory revolutionizes our understanding of the self by redefining the ego not as a mere mediator between desires and social norms, but as a dynamic, adaptable data processing center. This innovative approach positions the ego as an active agent capable of intentional growth and transformation, empowering individuals to consciously reprogram their mental and emotional responses to better align with their goals and values. Unlike traditional theories that often portray the ego as a static entity bound by unconscious drives, The New Ego Theory emphasizes its fluidity and the potential for self-directed evolution. By simplifying internal narratives and harnessing the power of cognitive flexibility, this theory offers practical tools for enhancing decision-making, fostering resilience, and ultimately, promoting a more profound and effective engagement with life's challenges. The New Ego Theory not only advances psychological science but also offers humanity a pathway to greater self-awareness, autonomy, and well-being.

1

THE ROLE OF DIVINEOS IN THE NEW EGO THEORY

Welcome to the gateway of a new understanding—one that redefines how we interact with our own minds and the soul potential that resides within us. The New Ego Theory, embedded within the DivineOS framework, offers humanity a powerful shift in how we view the ego, not as a mediator bound by archaic roles, but as a dynamic tool that allows us to reprogram our experiences, align with higher potential, and evolve through conscious choice.

DivineOS: An Operating System for Conscious Evolution

DivineOS, or "Divine Operating System," is a framework designed to upgrade the way we think, process, and experience reality. It's built around the premise that our mind, emotions, and spirit operate as an interconnected, programmable system—a system that can be refined, optimized, and upgraded to access higher levels of consciousness, clarity, and creativity. DivineOS provides tools, like choice commands and awareness sequences, that enable individuals to break free from limiting mental loops, emotional stagnation, and fear-based thought patterns. At its core, DivineOS is about reclaiming our mental architecture as a tool for personal mastery and aligning it with our higher purpose.

Main Components of DivineOS:

1. The 10 Dimensions of Awareness
Each dimension represents a layer or function of our awareness, from raw data intake to emotional processing to higher states of perception:

- **Speed**: Our natural capacity to process vast amounts of data in real time.
- **Storage**: The space where we store experiences, determining what we keep and what we release.
- **Story**: The narratives we create from our experiences and perceptions.
- **Senses**: Our sensory perceptions and how they feed into our understanding of reality.
- **Security**: The sense of inner safety that allows us to process experience without fear.
- **Soul**: Our inner source, providing guidance and connection to a larger spiritual purpose.
- **Subconscious**: The underlying patterns and beliefs that influence behavior.
- **System**: The internal structures and beliefs we rely on to process and make sense of life.
- **Seventh Sense**: A higher, multidimensional perception that integrates intuition.
- **Sphere**: Our unique field of creation, encompassing personal experience, reality, and potential.

2 Choice Commands
Choice commands are simple but powerful directives starting with "I choose..." that actively reprogram the mind by reinforcing conscious,

positive choices. Unlike affirmations, they function as direct commands to the subconscious, bypassing doubt and cultivating clear, non-distorted thinking.

3 The DivineOS Sequence Pattern Interrupt

The DivineOS sequence serves as a pattern interrupt, a technique to stop unproductive or negative thought loops in their tracks. By stating the sequence of dimensions (e.g., "Speed, Storage, Story, Senses, Security..."), users refocus their mind, regain self-command, and create space for high-vibrational states, like joy and clarity.

4 The Operating System Upgrade

This upgrade is a consistent practice of each three components of the tool - comprehension of how The 10 Dimensions of Awareness operates, The DivineOS Sequence, and Choice Commands - aligning thoughts, emotions, and intentions to achieve a clean, organized internal system. Through repetition of the sequence, individuals clear out unproductive mental loops and outdated narratives, making way for expansive thinking, creative action, and conscious evolution.

In summary, DivineOS is a practical, structured approach to understanding and optimizing our mental and emotional processing. It encourages a shift from reactionary, fear-based thinking to intentional, clear, and empowered self-leadership. Through the upgrade process, DivineOS guides individuals to experience life as conscious creators, continually refining their unique "operating system" to live in alignment with their higher purpose and potential.

Theory is powerful, but it becomes transformative when applied in practice. The New Ego Theory offers a set of tools and methods that allow individuals to consciously engage with their ego, reprogram their internal narratives, and align their behaviors with their highest potential. This chapter is dedicated to the practical applications of this theory, providing exercises and techniques to help you integrate these concepts into your everyday life.

Whether you're navigating challenges in relationships, seeking clarity in decision-making, or pursuing spiritual growth, the practical applications of The New Ego Theory can empower you to simplify your internal processes, make empowered choices, and accelerate your evolution.

Daily Reprogramming Ritual: Using Choice Commands

The foundation of practical application in The New Ego Theory is the use of choice commands. These intentional statements guide your ego's processing and help reprogram your mental landscape. One of the most effective ways to integrate choice commands into your life is through a daily reprogramming ritual.

Daily Reprogramming Ritual:

1. Morning Intention Setting: Start your day by selecting a specific series or single choice command that aligns with your goals or intentions for the day. For example:
    - "I choose clarity in my decisions."
    - "I choose to embrace abundance."
    - "I choose to approach challenges with confidence."
2. Say this command aloud or write it down in a journal. By doing this, you are programming your ego to process all the information it encounters that day through the lens of your chosen intention.
3. Mindful Practice Throughout the Day: As you go about your day, actively remind yourself of your choice command. When you encounter challenges or decisions, use your command to guide your thoughts and actions.
    - Example: If you encounter a stressful situation, remind yourself, "I choose calm and clarity," and notice how your ego shifts its processing to align with this directive.

4. Evening Reflection: At the end of the day, take a few moments to reflect on how your choice command influenced your thoughts and actions. Did you notice any shifts in your behavior or how you felt in your body? How did this intentional programming impact your day? Write your reflections in a journal to reinforce the effectiveness of the practice.

Why It Works: By engaging in a daily reprogramming ritual, you create consistency in how your ego processes information. This consistency strengthens the neural pathways associated with your choice commands, leading to lasting transformation over time.

Creating a Growth-Oriented Mindset: Simplifying Internal Narratives

Simplification is key to optimizing the ego's processing capacity. Many of us carry around complex internal narratives—stories about ourselves, our past, our limitations—that clutter our mental space and slow down growth.

A key practical application of The New Ego Theory is the process of simplifying internal narratives. This practice involves identifying and releasing overly complicated, conflicting, or outdated stories that no longer serve your highest potential.

Exercise: Simplifying Your Narrative

1. Identify Your Current Narrative: Take some time to write down the narratives you tell yourself in different areas of your life (e.g., career, relationships, self-worth). These could include statements like:
    - "I always struggle with success."
    - "Relationships are difficult for me."
    - "I'm not good enough to achieve my goals."

2. These narratives are often subtle but deeply embedded in our ego's processing system.
3. Challenge the Complexity: Once you've identified your current narratives, challenge the complexity of these stories. Are they rooted in past experiences that no longer apply? Are they creating unnecessary mental clutter?
4. Simplify and Replace: Choose to simplify these narratives by replacing them with clear, empowering statements. For example:
    - Replace "I always struggle with success" with "I choose to create success in my life."
    - Replace "Relationships are difficult for me" with "I choose to create meaningful, fulfilling relationships."
    - Replace "I'm not good enough" with "I choose to recognize my worth and pursue my goals with confidence."

Reinforce the New Narrative: Each time you catch yourself falling back into old narratives, consciously replace them with your simplified, empowering statements. Over time, this practice will reprogram your ego's processing, making it easier for you to operate from a place of clarity and self-empowerment.

DivineOS or Divine Operating System is more than a theory; it's a comprehensive framework designed to elevate our understanding of self and consciousness. Rooted in the principles of adaptability and intentionality, DivineOS operates as a personal operating system that empowers individuals to integrate the divine aspects of their being into daily life, creating pathways for growth, healing, and self-realization.

The Ego as the Central Processor in DivineOS

In the DivineOS, the ego is not an obstacle to be overcome or a burden to manage; it is the core processing center of your internal operating system. Think of it like the software that runs on powerful hardware—

your mind and body. The ego processes every piece of data that comes through your experiences, thoughts, emotions, and perceptions, synthesizing this information to help you navigate the material world.

But here's where The New Ego Theory flips the script: rather than just reacting to the data it's given—mediating desires and social norms—the ego can be consciously programmed. The New Ego Theory gives you the tools to decide how your ego processes that data. This means that instead of being caught in endless cycles of internal conflict or external pressure, your ego can be a force for growth, clarity, and transformation.

Imagine your soul potential as a vast source of energy and intelligence constantly feeding into your mind and body. The ego in DivineOS acts as the translator of this divine intelligence into actionable decisions, behaviors, and choices. Instead of feeling stuck in repetitive patterns or limited by fear and doubt, you can consciously direct the ego to process this divine energy and reflect it in your actions.

In traditional Freudian terms, the ego was viewed as a kind of mediator, managing the chaos of the id and the rigidity of the superego. While this was a breakthrough in understanding human psychology, it left the ego in a reactive position, always managing conflict. The New Ego Theory moves beyond this, giving the ego proactive power. It's not just negotiating between internal forces—it's actively shaping how those forces interact. The ego within DivineOS learns, adapts, and updates itself, just like an advanced AI, to bring you closer to your divine potential.

The Ego as a Bridge Between the Divine and Human Behavior

In the DivineOS, the ego is much more than a psychological construct; it becomes a bridge between soul potential and human action. You are not just a collection of thoughts, feelings, and experiences—you are also a vessel for something greater. The New Ego Theory helps you align your ego with this higher consciousness, transforming it from a survival mechanism into a tool for self-actualization and spiritual growth.

Where traditional views might see the ego as a barrier to higher spiritual awareness, the New Ego Theory sees it as the catalyst. It's the mechanism that allows you to take the abstract, ethereal concepts of the divine and manifest them into tangible results in your life. With this theory, you unlock the ego's true potential—using it to connect the gap between who you are now and the higher self you are meant to embody.

How The New Ego Theory Transforms Traditional Views

One of the key shifts that The New Ego Theory brings to the table is the move away from narrative-driven complexity. Traditional theories often see the ego as an entity entangled in stories—whether it's Freud's internal conflicts or Jung's archetypal fantasies. While these are fascinating frameworks, they lock us into narrative loops that can become difficult to break free from.

The New Ego Theory strips away these narratives and presents the ego as a functional tool. By viewing the ego as a dynamic data processor, you reduce the mental drag created by complex internal stories that don't serve your growth. You're no longer at the mercy of unconscious drives or inherited archetypes. Instead, you have a system that evolves based on how you choose to interact with it.

Why We Need The New Ego Theory

In today's world, where personal development and spiritual growth are often clouded by overwhelming complexity, The New Ego Theory offers a refreshing, grounded perspective. It simplifies the internal landscape without ignoring its richness. It gives you practical tools to consciously reprogram your ego, allowing you to evolve with ease and intentionality.

The truth is, human beings have an incredible capacity for growth—but we often find ourselves stuck in repetitive patterns because we're not equipped to rewire our core processing system, which is where The New Ego Theory comes in. It equips you with the understanding and tools you need to consciously shift your internal narrative, update your programming, and align your ego with the divine potential inside you.

In DivineOS, The New Ego Theory is not just about psychological healing—it's about accelerated evolution. It's about using the ego not as a mediator of conflict but as a powerful tool for unlocking your higher self.

As we step into the rest of the book, remember that the New Ego Theory redefines what the ego can be—transforming it from a reactive force to a dynamic tool of conscious evolution. Within the DivineOS framework, the ego isn't something to be transcended but embraced, refined, and aligned with your highest potential.

2

THE CORE TENETS OF THE NEW EGO THEORY

The ego. For centuries, it's been the center of countless debates in psychology, spirituality, and personal development. And yet, for all its scrutiny, the ego has often been misunderstood. Traditionally, it's been seen as a mediator between competing forces—our desires, morals, and the external world. In spiritual circles, it's frequently viewed as a hindrance to enlightenment. However, in The New Ego Theory, we see the ego not as something to be overcome or diminished, but as a powerful tool for conscious evolution.

The New Ego Theory introduces a radical shift in how we view the ego: as a dynamic, adaptable data processing center. This chapter explores the core principles of this theory, focusing on how the ego is a fluid system that can be reprogrammed through intentional choices and simplified internal narratives. By stripping away the complexity and seeing the ego as a system designed for growth, we unlock its potential to transform how we experience life.

A Dynamic, Adaptable Data Processor

In the past, the ego was often considered a fixed entity—part of our personality that develops early in life and remains relatively stable. Freud saw it as the mediator between the primal id and the moralistic superego. Jung placed it as part of a larger self, navigating the collective unconscious and archetypes. And while these theories have provided valuable insights into human behavior, they've limited the ego's role to a static or reactive force.

The New Ego Theory moves beyond this. Instead of being locked into a reactive or static position, the ego is viewed as a dynamic system, constantly processing internal and external data. This data includes your thoughts, emotions, and experiences, all of which are filtered through the ego and processed into actions and beliefs. The key difference is that in this new theory, you can actively choose how your ego processes this information.

Imagine your ego as your mind's central processing unit (CPU). It takes in data from every source—your environment, your emotions, your memories—and it processes this data to help you make decisions, form beliefs, and act in the world. But here's the exciting part: you can reprogram this processor. Unlike older models that saw the ego as bound by unconscious drives or societal norms, The New Ego Theory offers the possibility of conscious reprogramming.

Reprogramming the Ego: A New Approach to Growth

In traditional psychology, the ego is treated like a diplomat, a negotiator shuffling between the inner demands of our minds. We're told it's essential—an internal referee that mediates our psyche's conflicting voices. But what if that's just scratching the surface? What if that's all the ego has been allowed to be because we haven't dared to push its potential?

The New Ego Theory blows past this limiting idea. Here, the ego isn't some passive player juggling inner chaos. It's a potent, adaptable processor—one capable of total transformation, built to be reprogrammed by choice, by intention, by you. This isn't about reaction; it's about direction. It's about choosing the type of ego that best serves your highest potential and aligning it with that purpose, over and over, command by command.

Imagine this: instead of reacting to life based on old patterns, outdated fears, and learned limitations, your ego becomes a tool—one that's not just along for the ride but actively driving your evolution. You issue choice commands—clear, direct statements that don't just inspire, they recode. They are the instructions that bypass outdated programming and allow your ego to process each experience in a way that supports your growth, your truth, your mission.

Picture a life where you're not tripping over your past or tangled up in fear-based reactions, but moving forward with the ego as a finely tuned engine of conscious evolution.

In a sense, you become the programmer of your mind. By consciously selecting the data you feed into your ego and using specific choice commands, you can rewire how your ego processes information, making it more aligned with your desires, your growth, and your divine potential.

The Power of Intentionality: Choosing Your Internal Narrative

One of the most transformative aspects of The New Ego Theory is the emphasis on intentionality. In traditional models, the ego is often stuck in repetitive loops, reacting to external stimuli or internal conflicts based on past programming. The ego is seen as similar to a referee, constantly trying to balance competing forces.

In contrast, The New Ego Theory puts you in the driver's seat. Intentionality means that you can choose how your ego processes information. Rather than being at the mercy of unconscious drives or external pressures, you have the power to direct your ego in a way that serves your highest purpose. This is where the concept of simplifying internal narratives becomes crucial.

Simplification: The Key to Clarity and Growth

Humans tend to complicate their internal narratives. We create layers upon layers of stories, beliefs, and interpretations about ourselves and the world. These complex narratives can bog down the ego's processing capacity, creating mental drag. It's like trying to run a computer with too many programs open—everything slows down, and efficiency plummets.

The New Ego Theory teaches that simplification is key to unlocking the full potential of the ego. By reducing unnecessary complexity in your internal narrative, you free up cognitive resources that can be directed toward growth and evolution. When your internal story is simple, clear, and intentional, the ego can process data more efficiently, leading to better decision-making, reduced stress, and greater alignment with your goals.

For example, instead of saying, "I hope to be successful someday," a simplified and intentional command would be, "I choose to be successful now." This isn't just a linguistic shift—it's a reprogramming of how the ego processes your desire for success. By framing it as a choice, you empower your ego to align your thoughts, behaviors, and actions with that intention.

A question I find rarely being asked in self-development circles and spiritual teachings—where freeing oneself from the ego has become an obsession—is this: what do you actually hope to accomplish with this work?

Chasing down parts of you that "aren't really you" in order to discover what? A pristinely perceived identity and inner child entirely free of trauma, pain, and struggle? If so, let's consider: would that unblemished inner child even be equipped to operate at the level you desire in order to achieve your goals? Is it not more intriguing, even more empowering, to focus on building real skills, learning to create with tangible proof of your soul's potential—carrying with you all the strength, experience, and momentum you've already gained along the way?

Wouldn't it make more sense to meet the parts of yourself that you truly are by exploring what you can create and accomplish, rather than what you're "not"?

What do you think happens when you spend years chasing doorways labeled with "brokenness" and "healing"? Are you aware that your ego —like a hunting dog, loyal and skilled—will track exactly what you tell it to? Task it with clearing shadow, and your system will respond. Just like a computer program set to eradicate viruses, if there's no more malware to find, it doesn't just switch off. After you've invested so much time, energy, and conscious effort in identifying "viruses," you can be certain it will keep finding new insecurities, subtle fractures, some wound or problem for you to solve.

You've programmed it to do this. So you get precisely what you've trained it to find—and it won't stop delivering exactly that: more insecurity, more perceived brokenness, more problems to solve.

The ego's adaptability depends on the clarity of the data it processes. When you simplify your internal narratives and make intentional thought choices, you give your ego the tools it needs to evolve. This evolution is not just psychological—it's spiritual. By simplifying your mental processes and aligning them with your divine potential, you create a direct pathway to personal and spiritual growth.

In The New Ego Theory, the ego is no longer something to be battled or suppressed. It is a dynamic partner in your evolution, capable of transforming your internal and external realities through conscious choice, intentionality, and simplification.

Empowered Thought Choices: Rewiring the Ego for Success

A central tenet of The New Ego Theory is the functional mechanism of empowered thought choices. Every thought, belief, and narrative you hold is data that your ego processes. If you feed your ego limiting beliefs or self-defeating narratives, it will process and reinforce those patterns in your life. But if you consciously feed your ego choice-powered, growth-oriented thoughts, it will process and manifest those beliefs as your reality.

Consider the difference between saying "I am rich" versus "I choose to be rich." The first statement, "I am rich," is a declarative statement that might not resonate with your current reality. If you don't believe you are rich, the ego will experience cognitive dissonance, making it difficult to accept and process that statement. But "I choose to be rich" is an intentional choice, an empowered thought that the ego can process more easily. It frames wealth as something you are actively creating, rather than something you passively hope to become.

This subtle shift in language rewires the ego's processing system. It gives the ego a directive—a clear instruction to align your actions, decisions, and behaviors with the goal of becoming rich. Over time, as you reinforce these empowered choices, your ego becomes a powerful tool for manifesting your desires, creating a feedback loop that reinforces positive outcomes.

Words carry an immense, often underestimated power. They act as companions on our journey, shaping the way we connect with and relate to our own identity. The language we choose to describe our experiences can either dial us into a place of strength or, conversely, hold us in states of resistance and stagnation.

Consider the difference between choosing something and simply being dealt an "unfair hand" in life; this shift may seem subtle, but it has profound consequences.

When you choose growth, every part of your being—your energy, resilience, and inner fortitude—aligns with that intention. You aren't just adapting to circumstances; you're actively creating your own pathway. But when something is chosen for you, the options narrow: you either endure it, try to make the best of it, or find yourself rebelling against it.

Here's the hidden paradox: by resisting the idea that you're in charge of choosing your experience, you're actually choosing by default. This leaves you fighting an internal battle against the very mechanisms of your ego, stunting growth and keeping you locked in a teenage mindset —rebellious, but without a clear direction. Like a "rebel without a cause," this approach drains more of your potential than it builds.

So, what happens when you choose to take control of your language, framing your experiences as acts of choice rather than fate? You gain a self-directed, intentional force that doesn't just face life—it shapes it. This shift is not only liberating but transformative, guiding you to outgrow that internal rebellion and mature into a powerful, capable architect of your own identity.

As we move forward, we'll explore how deeper understanding of data processing awakens the architect within and supports our unique internal wiring. This releases us from the constraints of the heavy weight of processing data with speed by synthesizing embodied wisdom through a commitment to our inner rhythm.

3

REVOLUTIONIZING OUR UNDERSTANDING OF THE SELF

In The New Ego Theory, we're tossing out the stale idea that the ego is simply a middleman or a roadblock. It's time to recognize it for what it truly is: a dynamic, evolving data processor, adaptable and fully capable of aligning with our highest goals when we intentionally guide it.

By cutting through complicated inner stories and using empowered, precise commands, we can help our ego transform into a source of strength, clarity, and connection to the unique power within us. It's like training a personal helper in our mind to keep us focused, lift us up, and remind us of our own brilliance.

Let's get real—each leap in human progress has brought fresh theories and tools for understanding the mind, body, and soul. Yet, clinging to ideas that were relevant decades or centuries ago doesn't hold up against today's experience, insights, and technology. Imagine dragging the collective mind forward on ideas that suited a completely different era—it's irrational, painfully restrictive, and as outdated as trying to fuel a rocket with coal. Some truths are indeed timeless, holding strong through generations. But theories that haven't grown with us? They're dead weight we need to release if we want to accelerate at the speed we're meant for.

The reality is clear: if we keep filtering our minds through outdated concepts, we're not just slowing down—we're denying the potential we've been working so hard to reach. It's time to shape our mental frameworks around what we know now, not what was once assumed.

The Feedback Loop Between Ego and our higher Intelligence

In traditional psychological models, the ego is often seen as processing data in a one-way fashion—reacting to stimuli, mediating internal conflicts, and producing behavior. But within The New Ego Theory, the ego operates in a feedback loop with divine intelligence.

This feedback loop is essential to the functionality of DivineOS. Here's how it works:

1 Soul Potential and Divine Input: The ego receives signals from your higher consciousness—your divine potential. These signals can be spiritual impulses, desires, or intuitive nudges.

2 Ego Processing: The ego processes these signals, turning them into thoughts, decisions, and actions. It takes the boundless potential of the divine and translates it into real-world choices.

3 Human Action: The processed data (thoughts, decisions, actions) manifest in the physical world as behaviors, habits, and outcomes.

4 Feedback to the Full Spectrum System: The results of these actions are fed back into the ego, which assesses the success or alignment of these outcomes with the original divine intent. This feedback is then used to adjust future actions, continuously refining the ego's alignment with divine potential.

- Example: You might feel a nudge to start a new project or create something meaningful. Your ego processes this impulse, turning it into

3

REVOLUTIONIZING OUR UNDERSTANDING OF THE SELF

In The New Ego Theory, we're tossing out the stale idea that the ego is simply a middleman or a roadblock. It's time to recognize it for what it truly is: a dynamic, evolving data processor, adaptable and fully capable of aligning with our highest goals when we intentionally guide it.

By cutting through complicated inner stories and using empowered, precise commands, we can help our ego transform into a source of strength, clarity, and connection to the unique power within us. It's like training a personal helper in our mind to keep us focused, lift us up, and remind us of our own brilliance.

Let's get real—each leap in human progress has brought fresh theories and tools for understanding the mind, body, and soul. Yet, clinging to ideas that were relevant decades or centuries ago doesn't hold up against today's experience, insights, and technology. Imagine dragging the collective mind forward on ideas that suited a completely different era—it's irrational, painfully restrictive, and as outdated as trying to fuel a rocket with coal. Some truths are indeed timeless, holding strong through generations. But theories that haven't grown with us? They're dead weight we need to release if we want to accelerate at the speed we're meant for.

The reality is clear: if we keep filtering our minds through outdated concepts, we're not just slowing down—we're denying the potential we've been working so hard to reach. It's time to shape our mental frameworks around what we know now, not what was once assumed.

The Feedback Loop Between Ego and our higher Intelligence

In traditional psychological models, the ego is often seen as processing data in a one-way fashion—reacting to stimuli, mediating internal conflicts, and producing behavior. But within The New Ego Theory, the ego operates in a feedback loop with divine intelligence.

This feedback loop is essential to the functionality of DivineOS. Here's how it works:

1 Soul Potential and Divine Input: The ego receives signals from your higher consciousness—your divine potential. These signals can be spiritual impulses, desires, or intuitive nudges.

2 Ego Processing: The ego processes these signals, turning them into thoughts, decisions, and actions. It takes the boundless potential of the divine and translates it into real-world choices.

3 Human Action: The processed data (thoughts, decisions, actions) manifest in the physical world as behaviors, habits, and outcomes.

4 Feedback to the Full Spectrum System: The results of these actions are fed back into the ego, which assesses the success or alignment of these outcomes with the original divine intent. This feedback is then used to adjust future actions, continuously refining the ego's alignment with divine potential.

• Example: You might feel a nudge to start a new project or create something meaningful. Your ego processes this impulse, turning it into specific actions—researching, planning, taking the first steps. As you progress, the results of your actions feed back into your consciousness. If they align with your higher purpose, your ego reinforces those behaviors; if they don't, the ego adjusts, seeking greater alignment with your divine potential.

This continuous feedback loop allows the ego to evolve and grow, becoming more attuned to the divine signals it processes. In this way, the ego in DivineOS is a dynamic system that adapts and updates based on the flow of divine energy and the outcomes of human action.

Data Processing and Efficiency: Unlocking Cognitive Clarity

The ego's ability to process divine input depends heavily on the clarity of the data it receives. Just as a computer operates more efficiently when it's free from unnecessary processes, the ego functions optimally when it's free from mental clutter.

One of the central principles of The New Ego Theory is the importance of simplification in how the ego processes information. When we clutter the ego with complex narratives, conflicting beliefs, or unexamined fears, it slows down its ability to process divine input and hinders our ability to act with clarity.

This is where the power of intentionality and simplified internal narratives comes into play. By consciously choosing to focus on clear, empowering narratives, we reduce the cognitive load on the ego, allowing it to process data more efficiently.

- Example: Let's say you're facing a major life decision. If your ego is bogged down by fears, doubts, and conflicting beliefs about your capabilities, it will struggle to process the decision effectively. But if you simplify your internal narrative—by choosing empowering thoughts like "I choose to trust in my ability to succeed"—you free up cognitive resources, allowing the ego to process the decision with clarity and alignment.

In DivineOS, simplified internal narratives act as a form of mental optimization. By reducing the ego's need to process unnecessary or contradictory data, you increase its capacity to process divine input and translate it into meaningful action.

4

ORGANIZING THE EGO

The ego is like the operating system of your mind, managing input, sorting data, and running commands that shape your perception of reality. But in a world obsessed with either inflating or demonizing the ego, we've distorted its function, assigning it labels and roles it was never meant to have. Let's get clear: the ego is simply a function—a powerful, necessary one—that allows you to ask the most fundamental question: *Who am I?* The simplicity of this definition is a game changer. When understood and organized, the ego is the core operating system that lets you navigate life's complexities without distortion, freeing you to build a clear, empowered self.

Consider the ego as a system that verifies identity, much like a login prompt for a computer. It asks, *Is this you? Are you sure?* The ego fact-checks, compares, and aligns; it creates your sense of self and your awareness of separateness. But when the ego is mismanaged, when we mistake it for something sinister or malignant, it ends up running faulty programs, distorting your reality with self-doubt, self-criticism, and unnecessary competition.

The Ego as Identity Manager: The Power of Self-Awareness

At its best, the ego is like the identity software that makes sense of your unique being. It verifies your self-awareness, creating a necessary boundary between "you" and "other." And without this boundary, individuality—the foundation of creative expression and personal freedom—would not exist. Yet most people, conditioned by society, demonize the ego, thinking it's a barrier to enlightenment, a narcissistic influence, or a distortion that pulls us away from unity. But the ego's function isn't to distort; it's to differentiate. The ego gives you your unique perspective. It's the filter through which you can say, *I am me,* with clarity and conviction.

In this way, organizing the ego is simply about helping it do its job well—sorting the real from the distorted, seeing clearly what is true for you, and releasing the irrelevant. When the ego is organized, you understand that it's there to question, to reflect, to fact-check. And when it does this correctly, you get a clear, accurate picture of yourself in relation to the world around you.

Misalignment and Distortion: The Ego Under False Input

Problems arise when the ego processes distorted information—external programs like societal expectations, cultural narratives, or false metrics of success. Imagine feeding a computer virus-laden software. The system doesn't fail because it's inherently flawed; it fails because it's been compromised by low-quality input. Similarly, when the ego measures itself against distorted standards, it builds a distorted self-concept.

Take societal programming around success. From childhood, many are taught that value lies in comparison, in winning, in climbing over others to prove worth. If the ego internalizes this program, it begins to run loops of inadequacy, never satisfied, always seeking external validation. The result? A reactive, insecure self-concept. But when the ego is organized, it no longer feeds off distorted programs; instead, it becomes a sharp, clear instrument that enables you to see your own depth and stand in your own power.

The Key to Self-Mastery: Organizing the Ego to Know Thyself

Organizing the ego requires awareness of these external programs and deciding to process only high-quality input. When you clean up the programs influencing your ego, you release reactive emotions and distorted identities. This process turns the ego inward, allowing it to ask more constructive questions: *What do I truly value? Who am I beyond societal measures?* The ego, functioning properly, stops reacting to external distortions and instead starts creating a self based on internal truth.

Imagine a mirror. If it's covered in smudges and cracks, the reflection will be inaccurate. But if it's clean and clear, you see yourself precisely as you are. Similarly, when you organize the ego, it stops projecting fears and doubts based on distorted realities and begins to reflect the truth of who you are. This process is revolutionary. When you stop running distorted programming through your ego, you end up with a clear, empowered identity, unshaken by external judgments or validation.

The Ego's Role in Creation: Using Your Identity as a Platform

An organized ego is not just a tool for self-awareness; it's a platform for creation. When the ego is aligned, it doesn't just identify who you are—it becomes the framework through which you can create the life you want. Rather than spending energy on comparison or insecurity, the organized ego channels that energy toward building, creating, evolving. In this state, the ego doesn't need approval or fear judgment; it operates from a place of clarity and purpose.

The ego, functioning as intended, recognizes its boundaries but doesn't suffer them. It knows it is both a part of the "all" and yet distinct within that all—a unique piece of the whole, like a single glass of water drawn from the ocean. Yes, it shares the same essence as the ocean, but it has its own purpose, its own containment, its own reason for being. The organized ego isn't threatened by this paradox; it thrives within it.

Correcting Distortion: Filtering Reality Through Accurate Awareness

With an organized ego, you stop taking in distorted reflections of yourself from society's performance metrics, power games, or provision systems. Instead, you recognize those systems for what they are—default programs, not ultimate truths. The ego's role is to ask questions, and it will always seek answers. But when the ego processes information accurately, it asks questions that lead to genuine insight rather than unnecessary self-criticism.

By organizing the ego, you stop processing inaccurate input, thereby freeing up cognitive and emotional resources for things that matter. This clarity allows you to respond to life from a place of depth, rather than reacting from surface-level insecurities or fears. The ego, in its organized state, becomes a tool that sharpens your focus, heightens your self-awareness, and grounds you in an empowered identity.

Creating from the Core: The Ego as an Expression of Divine Individuality

The beauty of an organized ego is that it frees you to create from your essence. No longer distracted by distorted beliefs, you're able to operate from a pure sense of individuality—an individuality that is part of the whole but distinct in its expression. The organized ego knows itself as a creator. It understands that it has the ability, the right, and the power to shape reality according to its own inner truth.

Through the lens of an organized ego, high vibrational emotions—joy, peace, creativity—arise naturally, not as forced positivity but as genuine responses to your alignment. This is not about ego-inflation;

it's about clarity. You become a co-creator with the universe, fueled by your unique frequency, in partnership with your soul's purpose. You're not asking external reality to validate you; you're creating a reality that reflects your own value back to you.

Choice Commands: Directing the Ego with Intention

Choice commands are the essential tools for organizing the ego. These are not affirmations; they're intentional directives that execute divine will. Each choice command begins with *"I choose"* and acts as a filter, directing the ego to process experiences in alignment with your highest intentions.

Examples of choice commands include:

- *"I choose to see this experience as a reflection of my potential, free from my limitations."*

- *"I choose to focus on what serves my purpose, releasing distractions."*

- *"I choose clarity over distortion, truth over fear."*

Using choice commands is like giving your ego a roadmap, instructing it to process incoming information with precision and focus. Each command is a conscious decision that removes the reactive programming and aligns the ego with your core truth. Over time, this practice reorients the ego from a fearful, fragmented processor to a clear, confident guide.

PART II
DATA PROCESSING

Let's get one thing straight: your mind is a data-processing powerhouse. It's handling inputs from every angle—thoughts, emotions, sensations, memories—while somehow keeping you from losing it over the constant flow. DivineOS? Think of it as the mental upgrade you didn't know you needed, a re-imagined operating system that doesn't just sort your thoughts and keep you functioning but actually primes you to take control.

Here's the gist: DivineOS takes the wayward wanderings and background chaos of your mind and organizes them with purpose. Forget the days when your ego ran rogue, cluttering up your thoughts with old insecurities and baggage. DivineOS is like switching your brain from basic survival mode to boosted creation mode, where each process—each thought, memory, and response—is aligned with what you actually want to create and experience in life.

This isn't just about a smoother ride; it's about firing on all cylinders. The moment you start using it, DivineOS becomes the "choose your own adventure" control panel for your consciousness, so you can stop reacting to life and start designing it.

5

DATA PROCESSING

The DivineOS functions much like a high-performance computer operating system, organizing and optimizing human consciousness to process information, make decisions, and operate seamlessly. Here's a breakdown of the analogy:

1. **Input Processing (Speed and Storage)** Just as a computer receives and rapidly processes input from various sources (keyboard, mouse, software), DivineOS enables the mind to handle the vast amount of incoming sensory data, thoughts, and emotions with efficiency. The "Speed" dimension manages this high-speed input flow, while "Storage" organizes experiences, storing useful information and discarding irrelevant data to prevent cognitive overload.
2. **File Management (Story and Senses)** Computers label and categorize data files, creating meaning and access paths for efficient retrieval. In DivineOS, the "Story" dimension labels experiences, assigning them meaning within the user's inner framework, while "Senses" act as live detectors, assessing the current state and aligning or correcting emotional responses in real time.

3. **Security Protocols (Security and Soul)** Just as an OS runs security protocols to protect against viruses and unauthorized access, DivineOS includes "Security" as a built-in system that recognizes threats to inner harmony, like limiting beliefs or negative emotions. "Soul" acts as the deeper, self-regenerative core, much like a secure OS backup, ensuring that all functions return to a stable, aligned state.
4. **Background Processing (Subconscious and Systems)** A computer constantly runs background processes to keep things running smoothly, handling complex operations the user may not see. DivineOS uses "Subconscious" as the foundational background process, carrying out habitual patterns until they're intentionally updated. "Systems" serve as operational configurations that define how thoughts, beliefs, and routines run automatically in the background, maintaining stability and enabling daily function.
5. **Enhanced Processing Mode (Seventh Sense and Sphere)** Much like a computer in "boost mode," DivineOS activates the "Seventh Sense"—a combination of all senses plus intuition that elevates decision-making and awareness into a higher, unified intelligence. The "Sphere" then operates like a virtual reality environment, where the user's reality reflects the input from their choices, much as a VR system creates a customized experience based on program settings.

In essence, DivineOS upgrades the mind's processing power, security, and output, aligning each function to serve the user's highest potential. Like a computer system, DivineOS is structured to make information processing not only efficient but also aligned with the user's intentional commands, optimizing consciousness to enhance life experiences.

5

DATA PROCESSING

The DivineOS functions much like a high-performance computer operating system, organizing and optimizing human consciousness to process information, make decisions, and operate seamlessly. Here's a breakdown of the analogy:

1. **Input Processing (Speed and Storage)** Just as a computer receives and rapidly processes input from various sources (keyboard, mouse, software), DivineOS enables the mind to handle the vast amount of incoming sensory data, thoughts, and emotions with efficiency. The "Speed" dimension manages this high-speed input flow, while "Storage" organizes experiences, storing useful information and discarding irrelevant data to prevent cognitive overload.
2. **File Management (Story and Senses)** Computers label and categorize data files, creating meaning and access paths for efficient retrieval. In DivineOS, the "Story" dimension labels experiences, assigning them meaning within the user's inner framework, while "Senses" act as live detectors, assessing the current state and aligning or correcting emotional responses in real time.

3. **Security Protocols (Security and Soul)** Just as an OS runs security protocols to protect against viruses and unauthorized access, DivineOS includes "Security" as a built-in system that recognizes threats to inner harmony, like limiting beliefs or negative emotions. "Soul" acts as the deeper, self-regenerative core, much like a secure OS backup, ensuring that all functions return to a stable, aligned state.
4. **Background Processing (Subconscious and Systems)** A computer constantly runs background processes to keep things running smoothly, handling complex operations the user may not see. DivineOS uses "Subconscious" as the foundational background process, carrying out habitual patterns until they're intentionally updated. "Systems" serve as operational configurations that define how thoughts, beliefs, and routines run automatically in the background, maintaining stability and enabling daily function.
5. **Enhanced Processing Mode (Seventh Sense and Sphere)** Much like a computer in "boost mode," DivineOS activates the "Seventh Sense"—a combination of all senses plus intuition that elevates decision-making and awareness into a higher, unified intelligence. The "Sphere" then operates like a virtual reality environment, where the user's reality reflects the input from their choices, much as a VR system creates a customized experience based on program settings.

In essence, DivineOS upgrades the mind's processing power, security, and output, aligning each function to serve the user's highest potential. Like a computer system, DivineOS is structured to make information processing not only efficient but also aligned with the user's intentional commands, optimizing consciousness to enhance life experiences.

6

MULTIDIMENSIONAL DATABASES

Your mind is more than a string of thoughts. Think of it as a multidimensional database—a system pulling in countless points of data, not just from the world around you, but from the complex architecture within. This isn't just another layer to add to your inner world; it's an entire dimension waiting to be unlocked, upgraded, and optimized. Here, you aren't just thinking—you're moving beyond linear thought into something far more expansive and strategic.

We've spent so much time letting outdated thought systems call the shots. We've stuck to rigid, flat planes of thinking, reacting to patterns that no longer serve us. But this isn't a linear world anymore, and your mind? It's made for multidimensional data. Information hits us in torrents now, and in the age of constant connectivity, we're not only sifting through vast amounts of external input; we're diving into the depths of our internal landscape, where intuition and instinct lie in wait.

So, what is a multidimensional database in this context? It's a framework—a cube if you will—that lets you organize all of this input from multiple directions, a place where data isn't just categorized but intuitively processed, optimized for your highest intelligence. Think of it as the soul's way of running a high-performance system, with you as both architect and operator.

The Cube of Consciousness

Picture it: each face of this mental cube represents a different aspect of your experience—emotions, logic, intuition, memory, awareness. Data flows in and is immediately sorted into each of these facets. It doesn't bog you down. It doesn't create clutter. Instead, it becomes fuel for a higher state of processing. You get to take command of this system, to define the parameters through which your experiences are processed, giving you authority over what you think, how you feel, and ultimately, how you choose.

In this chapter, you're not just learning to manage thoughts. You're learning to lead them. The database you're building isn't static; it evolves, powered by the choices you make and the awareness you cultivate. This is about setting up a system within you that can move beyond reaction and into creation—a system that aligns your sensitivity with intelligence, making you the authority of your internal landscape.

Self-Leadership Through Higher Intelligence

When you start organizing your mind as a multidimensional database, you're stepping into a position of self-leadership. You're saying, "I choose how information moves through me." This act alone frees you from old, limiting cycles of thought and opens up new levels of clarity and potential. You're giving yourself permission to release what's no longer useful, to streamline your mental flow, and to upgrade from outdated modes of thinking.

And this isn't about "positive thinking" or mantras that crumble the moment they're tested. This is about restructuring the way you process information from the ground up. You're rewiring your ego to operate as the soul's ally, not its opponent. You're mastering the ability to command and reprogram fear, to root your choices in a deep, stable awareness that cuts through the noise and empowers your inner essence.

Commanding the Middle Pillar

Within this multidimensional framework, you'll find the core—the middle pillar. This pillar represents balance, the calm eye of the storm where heaven and hell converge, where suffering meets triumph. This is where you take control of your energy, your attention, and your awareness, cultivating the courage to face both your shadows and your highest aspirations. You are neither running from the low vibrations nor clinging to the highs. You are the one in control, steering with a clear mind and a steady hand.

So, here's the invitation: step into the multidimensional database of your mind. Define it, direct it, and let it run. Take ownership of this vast terrain within you. Let it fuel your growth, sharpen your awareness, and make space for the untapped potential that's been waiting all along. You're not just a participant in your own mind; you're the architect, the programmer, the leader of a system designed to process, transform, and create in ways that are uniquely yours. Welcome to the future of thinking—where every piece of data is an opportunity for elevation.

7

AUTHORITY AND SELF LEADING THE OPERATING SYSTEM

Imagine this: You wake up one morning feeling the same relentless undercurrent of frustration and exhaustion. The world looks the same, but something feels like it's pressing on you, a dull weight in your chest, a whisper that you're circling in place. You've done everything right, followed the scripts handed to you by society, education, and maybe even self-help books that promised transformation, but here you are—stuck. It's like standing at the edge of a wilderness you can't quite see, yet you sense it's there. A place inside yourself that holds answers, direction, even a kind of freedom, but somehow, it feels out of reach.

Maybe you can feel it right now: that pull toward something greater, a potential you can almost touch. But the thoughts in your head? They keep circling back to the same places. You think, "What if I'm just not built for the life I want? What if this friction is just...me?"

Now picture this—the mind as a vast network of highways, roads, and dead ends. For most of your life, you've driven the same narrow paths, thinking they're the only ones. You follow the grooves worn by years of habit, self-doubt, and survival. But what if these aren't the only routes available? What if there's a way to rewrite the map, to command your mind to build new roads, create new landscapes, lead you into territories you haven't even imagined?

These concepts aren't here to show you how to cope with the roads you already know. They're here to hand you the keys to a whole new operating system, one that puts you firmly in the driver's seat. We're not talking about positive thinking, mantras, or "fake it till you make it" affirmations that feel hollow. This is about dismantling the default settings of your mind—the reactive loops, the limiting beliefs, the habits that have quietly decided your life for you—and choosing, consciously, what kind of mind you want to live with.

The journey of self-leadership begins with that decision: to confront the default, to meet the parts of yourself that feel unchangeable and expand beyond them. You have the tools within you. You have the potential to lead, to architect your thoughts, emotions, and responses. DivineOS isn't here to hand you answers on a silver platter; it's here to invite you into a mastery of your own mind, to make you the designer of an internal world that finally reflects the life you want.

So, as you read on, ask yourself—what if today was the day you stopped being led by old scripts and took the reins instead? What if you stepped fully into the role of the architect, the creator, the one who decides which paths to carve and which to leave behind? The choice is yours.

Every step you take within your mind is an unfolding realization—a dialogue where consciousness meets itself and learns its own depth. In this journey, thoughts and memories aren't just fleeting; they're like guideposts, showing you the inner framework of who you are and who you can become. Unlike the traditional approach to mindset work, which often relies on recycling positivity or "managing" thoughts, this isn't about taming your mind. It's about inviting it to operate at its full intelligence, free from constraints.

If we simply ask the mind to stay in line or play nice, it's like sticking a genius in a classroom that never moves beyond basic math. There's no stimulation, no depth, nothing to engage with, and so it seeks outlets—rebelling, numbing out, or getting lost in distraction. But give your mind a challenge worthy of its power, an intentional system that speaks to its potential, and watch it come alive. This journey calls on every part of you to engage, not just conform. It's not about becoming better within the limits of an outdated paradigm; it's about realizing that those limits were never real to begin with.

Let's be clear: you're not the problem. The paradigm is. What we focus on is. It's time to engage with the inner landscape through intelligent concepts and purposeful intention, directing your mind in a way that makes growth inevitable.

At this level, it's not enough to let the mind run on autopilot. To lead your operating system is to define the parameters by which thoughts, emotions, and intuition flow through you. Each layer, each decision point, becomes part of a carefully crafted system, an internal structure where you hold the reins. Here, you're stepping up as both architect and operator, using the Divine Operating System (DivineOS) to create a coherent framework for your inner world. DivineOS isn't just a metaphor; it's a practice, a series of commands that position you as the creator of your experience.

DivineOS: A Journey Through Ten Dimensions of Awareness

DivineOS brings together ten dimensions of awareness, each acting as a pillar within your mental landscape. We call this sequence the *Divine Command Sequence*—a roadmap that directs you through layers of thought, feeling, intuition, and experience. It's a tool for grounding, a tool for clarity, and, above all, a tool for command. Here's the sequence again:

Speed, Storage, Story, Senses, Security, Soul, Subconscious, Systems, Seventh Sense, Sphere.

Each word is a doorway, a reminder of the dynamics within your mind. When recited aloud, this sequence pulls your awareness into each layer, activating every part of your operating system to work together with cohesion and purpose. Think of it as the heartbeat of DivineOS, a pulse that aligns each part of your mind.

Breaking Down the Journey

The journey through DivineOS isn't just about memorizing words; it's about exploring how each layer functions within you.

- **Speed**: This is the pace at which information flows. With awareness of speed, you're in tune with the intensity of data entering your system, deciding when to slow down and when to let information move freely.
- **Storage**: Not every piece of information needs to linger. Self-leadership means choosing what stays, what goes, and what serves your greater purpose.
- **Story**: Data becomes experience when we give it meaning. Here, you choose the narratives you wish to keep and rewrite those that no longer align with who you are becoming.
- **Senses**: Beyond the physical, your senses include intuition, awareness, and emotional insight. This layer allows you to interact with the world on a multidimensional level, a balance between sensing and creating.
- **Security**: Here lie the fear programs and survival instincts. You're not here to shut them down; you're here to lead them, ensuring that safety is an ally rather than a cage.
- • **Soul**: At the core, your soul holds your blueprint, the vision that drives you. This is the dimension that brings purpose to every layer of your mind, aligning all parts of your system with a deeper calling.

- **Subconscious**: Beneath the surface lies a reservoir of past programming. Self-leadership invites you to bring subconscious patterns into conscious awareness, transforming them into tools for growth.
- **Systems**: This layer encompasses the habits, frameworks, and patterns that shape your experience. As the leader, you define these systems, deciding how they support the life you're building.
- **Seventh Sense**: The seventh sense is heightened awareness, the convergence of all dimensions. When active, this sense allows for a unified, intuitive experience where mind, body, and soul work in seamless harmony.
- **Sphere**: This is the culmination, the full expanse of your internal landscape, the universe that you stand upon. It's the ground on which you build, the totality of your system in alignment.

From Command to Choice

Once you've anchored this sequence within you, each layer of DivineOS becomes an active choice, not a default setting. Self-leading your operating system means more than simply acknowledging these layers; it means crafting commands—conscious choices—that direct how each part of your mind operates. When you recite the Command Sequence, you're not just grounding yourself; you're affirming the parameters through which you process, perceive, and respond. This shift from passive reaction to active command is the core of self-leadership, a practice of engaging fully with every dimension of your operating system.

In a moment of stress, instead of getting caught in loops or overwhelmed by thought spirals, you can call on the Command Sequence. This brings you back to center, grounding you in your ability to lead, not just feel. Through DivineOS, you're continuously reprogramming yourself from survival-based reactions to creation-based choices. It's a transformation that goes beyond self-awareness into active, conscious mastery.

Waking the Architect

Leading your operating system isn't about perfecting or fixing yourself; it's about remembering your role as the architect of your mental landscape. The Divine Command Sequence is a tool for sovereignty, for awakening the part of you that isn't afraid to lead, to rewrite, and to create anew. With DivineOS, your mind becomes a canvas, each layer a brushstroke that you control.

In the end, the purpose of DivineOS is to bring you to a state of unshakable authority. You're not at the mercy of old narratives, fear-based responses, or subconscious loops. You are leading them, using every dimension of awareness as a tool to shape the life you're here to create. The journey through DivineOS is one of self-mastery, an invitation to claim your role as the conscious force within your own mind.

With this practice, you are stepping into the power to direct, transform, and align every part of your internal universe. You're not just experiencing life; you're actively building it, commanding each layer of your mind with purpose, intention, and an unbreakable sense of self-leadership. Welcome to the journey.

8

DYNAMIC FIELDS OF INFORMATION: UNIQUE WIRING AND NEURODIVERGENT SENSITIVITY

In the DivineOS framework, high sensitivity and overwhelm are not seen as obstacles but as essential pathways through which our unique systems process information. According to the new ego theory, the ego acts as a vigilant gatekeeper, constantly scanning for safety and assessing the world based on our past experiences and perceived risks. Often, this process occurs without our awareness, defaulting us into fear-based states that limit our potential. When we bring conscious awareness to this, we realize that input, processing, and output are dynamic flows, meant to be engaged with our full presence.

By attuning ourselves to this flow, we take on the role of steward within the DivineOS, recognizing that high sensitivity is simply one channel through which the world moves within us. Embracing this perspective allows us to recalibrate the ego's response, transforming it from a mere fact-checker into a guide for growth. In this way, we harness our DivineOS as a pathway for deeper awareness, resilience, and personal evolution, allowing our neurodivergent minds to thrive rather than merely survive.

High Sensitivity and DivineOS: Reframing Overwhelm Through New Ego Theory

Picture this: you're standing in the center of a bustling marketplace. People press in from all sides, voices pile up like layers of static, colors flash, and the air is thick with the smells of food, smoke, sweat. Every sensation bombards you. The noise is a wall, the lights are searing, and every small movement around you registers like an electric shock. You try to focus, try to find a path through, but there's too much happening, too much to process, too much information demanding your attention all at once. You're overwhelmed, overstimulated, and ready to escape.

Now, let's be real: for the neurodivergent, modern life can often feel just like this. But the message society hands you is simple: "You're sensitive. You're anxious. Maybe you just can't handle the pace." And there it is—the label, the brush-off, the tidy little box that tries to define you. You start believing that maybe it's a flaw, that you're missing some essential gene for calm and focus. But what if that sense of overwhelm isn't a weakness? What if it's not that you're feeling *too much*, but rather that you're processing *more*?

This is the truth about neurodivergent wiring: it's not that you're built wrong; it's that you're tuned to a different frequency. What feels overwhelming is actually your mind's ability to take in vast amounts of information, to sense more, to register subtleties that most people miss entirely. It's not a flaw; it's a superpower. But raw sensitivity, without structure, can feel like chaos. The question isn't whether you're too sensitive; it's how you can turn that sensitivity into a dynamic field of creation.

Knowing Your Unique Wiring: The First Step in Self-Mastery

For the neurodivergent mind, the world's one-size-fits-all blueprint doesn't work. Your wiring is unique, a system that thrives on depth, pattern recognition, and nonlinear thinking. Instead of forcing yourself to adopt conventional structures—daily journaling, rigid routines,

8

DYNAMIC FIELDS OF INFORMATION: UNIQUE WIRING AND NEURODIVERGENT SENSITIVITY

In the DivineOS framework, high sensitivity and overwhelm are not seen as obstacles but as essential pathways through which our unique systems process information. According to the new ego theory, the ego acts as a vigilant gatekeeper, constantly scanning for safety and assessing the world based on our past experiences and perceived risks. Often, this process occurs without our awareness, defaulting us into fear-based states that limit our potential. When we bring conscious awareness to this, we realize that input, processing, and output are dynamic flows, meant to be engaged with our full presence.

By attuning ourselves to this flow, we take on the role of steward within the DivineOS, recognizing that high sensitivity is simply one channel through which the world moves within us. Embracing this perspective allows us to recalibrate the ego's response, transforming it from a mere fact-checker into a guide for growth. In this way, we harness our DivineOS as a pathway for deeper awareness, resilience, and personal evolution, allowing our neurodivergent minds to thrive rather than merely survive.

High Sensitivity and DivineOS: Reframing Overwhelm Through New Ego Theory

Picture this: you're standing in the center of a bustling marketplace. People press in from all sides, voices pile up like layers of static, colors flash, and the air is thick with the smells of food, smoke, sweat. Every sensation bombards you. The noise is a wall, the lights are searing, and every small movement around you registers like an electric shock. You try to focus, try to find a path through, but there's too much happening, too much to process, too much information demanding your attention all at once. You're overwhelmed, overstimulated, and ready to escape.

Now, let's be real: for the neurodivergent, modern life can often feel just like this. But the message society hands you is simple: "You're sensitive. You're anxious. Maybe you just can't handle the pace." And there it is—the label, the brush-off, the tidy little box that tries to define you. You start believing that maybe it's a flaw, that you're missing some essential gene for calm and focus. But what if that sense of overwhelm isn't a weakness? What if it's not that you're feeling *too much*, but rather that you're processing *more*?

This is the truth about neurodivergent wiring: it's not that you're built wrong; it's that you're tuned to a different frequency. What feels overwhelming is actually your mind's ability to take in vast amounts of information, to sense more, to register subtleties that most people miss entirely. It's not a flaw; it's a superpower. But raw sensitivity, without structure, can feel like chaos. The question isn't whether you're too sensitive; it's how you can turn that sensitivity into a dynamic field of creation.

Knowing Your Unique Wiring: The First Step in Self-Mastery

For the neurodivergent mind, the world's one-size-fits-all blueprint doesn't work. Your wiring is unique, a system that thrives on depth, pattern recognition, and nonlinear thinking. Instead of forcing yourself to adopt conventional structures—daily journaling, rigid routines, forced positivity—it's about creating a framework that respects and enhances how *you* process.

Let's break this down with a simple example: sensitivity to noise. For you, the ticking of a clock, distant laughter, or even a soft hum from a neighboring room might disrupt your focus, splintering your thoughts. The world says you need to "toughen up," but the truth is, this sensitivity is an ability to tune in deeply to every layer of your environment. Knowing this about yourself isn't a limitation; it's an invitation to master your surroundings, to create spaces that foster your genius.

When you understand this sensitivity as part of your wiring, you gain the tools to build your environment with intention. You can establish a dynamic field of creation—a personal framework that aligns with how you naturally operate. Instead of feeling bound by traditional steps to "get in the zone," you'll begin to see yourself as a powerful conduit, tuned to high sensitivity. The trick isn't to dampen the signal; it's to channel it.

The Depth Dimensions of Reality: Creating Your Own Field

Most conventional advice on creation and manifestation is as restrictive as it is prescriptive. You're told to journal daily, visualize outcomes, or repeat affirmations as if they're magic spells that'll unlock your potential. But when you're wired differently, those rules often lead to frustration or disconnect. What you need isn't a script but a map of your inner landscape—a way to access the unique dimensions of creation that exist inside of you.

These dimensions are aspects of creation that work with, rather than against, your wiring. They're not rigid steps but rather dynamic elements of focus that let you navigate your inner world. Instead of blindly adopting popular techniques, you learn how creation flows through *you*, tuning into the patterns and dimensions that resonate with your specific makeup. For example, you may discover that journaling works not because it's a required ritual, but because it grounds your thoughts in a way that clarifies your energy. It's about knowing the *why* behind each practice, and letting your intuition guide you to what genuinely aligns.

Dynamic Creation Through Self-Understanding

When you embrace your unique wiring, you stop wasting time on methods that don't fit. You no longer need to mold yourself to external rules that ignore the complexity of your mind. Creation becomes a personal art, shaped by your understanding of what your wiring can do when given the space and freedom to thrive.

You are not sensitive. You are aware. You don't "struggle to focus"—you just need the right landscape to thrive in. And your ability to process more data isn't a burden; it's the path to mastery, if you know how to wield it. By stepping into this field of dynamic creation, you become the master of your own system, building a life that aligns not with the status quo, but with the vast, extraordinary power of your own mind.

9

CRAFTING YOUR ENVIRONMENT AND ALIGNING WITH YOUR INNER RHYTHM

It starts in the quiet spaces, those subtle moments where you feel the tension creep up, where the clutter, noise, and sheer busyness of life accumulate and weigh you down. You know that feeling —the one that nags at you, like a low hum in the background, making you restless, scattered, and drained. You tell yourself it's just stress or that you're "sensitive," that maybe the chaos of the world is simply too much. But what if I told you that what you're feeling is something more?

For those with neurodivergent wiring, the world isn't just overwhelming; it's amplified. Every sight, sound, texture, and interaction pulses through you at a higher volume, registering in ways others might not notice. It's not a flaw or something to be numbed. This heightened sensitivity is a gift. But to unlock its power, to channel it into true mastery, you have to create a space where your mind and body can thrive—a physical and mental sanctuary that aligns with your unique rhythm.

The Power of Physical Space: Clearing Clutter to Clear the Mind

Think of your environment as the canvas on which your creativity, energy, and potential come to life. Just as stagnant water becomes murky, a cluttered or neglected space stagnates your mental clarity. For a highly sensitive person, physical clutter becomes emotional clutter; messes in your environment have a way of creeping into your mind, taking up precious space in your thoughts, weighing on your focus.

Creating an environment that aligns with your rhythm doesn't mean having a showroom-perfect space, nor does it mean obsessing over keeping every inch pristine. It's about consciously managing the energy of the space, clearing away anything that weighs you down, and introducing elements that lift you up. Something as simple as opening windows, clearing out piles of clutter, changing the bedding, or even vacuuming the floors can shift the energy in your environment, creating a blank canvas for creativity and focus.

Think of it like tending to a garden. The act of cleaning, moving, organizing isn't just about order; it's a form of energetic maintenance. The intention behind every action is to cultivate a space where your unique mind can flourish. This isn't about perfection; it's about creating flow, about removing obstacles that snag your attention and keep you from sinking deeply into your creative work.

Aligning with Your Inner Rhythm: Following Your Own Clock

Once your environment is aligned, the next step is to tune into the rhythm within you. For neurodivergent minds, conventional schedules can feel like a constant battle, as though you're living on someone else's clock. The world says work from 9 to 5, eat three meals a day, and sleep eight hours every night. But maybe your mind comes alive at 2 a.m., or you feel most creative after a nap in the afternoon. You're not broken; you're just wired differently.

When you give yourself permission to follow your inner rhythm, you're removing the pressure to conform to a clock that was never designed for you. You're letting your body and mind dictate when it's time to rest, create, or focus, trusting that your internal timing knows better than any external schedule. Start small: notice when you naturally feel energized, when you're pulled to rest, when your creative ideas flow most easily. As you let yourself lean into these rhythms, you'll discover that the world doesn't collapse when you listen to your own clock—it expands.

And yes, at first, this can feel indulgent or even frightening. You may find yourself needing extra rest, perhaps even "catching up" on years of pushing against your body's signals. Think of this as a reset, a way of rebalancing after years of running on someone else's terms. You're building a relationship with yourself, proving over time that you'll honor what your body and mind truly need. Once you get through this recalibration, you'll find yourself naturally falling into a rhythm that not only feels good but also fuels your productivity and creativity.

The Magic of Movement: Shifting Energy in Your Space and Life

Creating a dynamic flow of energy is the final key to aligning your environment and rhythm. Stagnant energy is like stale air—it weighs on you, slows you down, and dampens inspiration. This applies to both your physical space and your mental space. Just as cleaning and reorganizing can lift the energy in a room, regularly moving your body and shifting your work location can refresh your mind.

If you work from home, try working in different rooms, changing your perspective, or even stepping out to a café. Bring a sense of movement into your routine, and you'll notice the difference in your mental clarity and focus. Movement breaks up the energetic buildup that occurs in places where we spend too much time in one spot. Think of it like clearing out the cobwebs, not just in your house but in your mind.

The beauty of this process is that it's entirely within your control. You get to decide how your space looks, feels, and functions. You get to design your schedule based on what fuels you. Every choice you make, every intentional action, moves you closer to a state of mastery—where the magic of creation flows naturally from your alignment with your own rhythm and the world around you.

Moving Toward Mastery: Creating a Life That Works for You

Mastering your physical environment and inner rhythm is about creating a life that supports your unique wiring rather than working against it. When you align your surroundings and rhythm, you're building a foundation where your sensitivity becomes a powerful tool for creation. This alignment doesn't just make life easier; it empowers you to tap into a deep well of creativity and focus, a space where your mind and body work in harmony.

This is where magic lives: in the small, intentional choices that shift your reality, in the act of claiming your right to a life designed for you. There's a path forward that honors every part of you, every quirk, every sensitivity, every unique aspect of your mind. Take responsibility for your space. Honor your rhythm. And as you do, you'll step into a mastery that doesn't conform—it commands.

PART III
THE MIND VIRUS

10

FEAR IS A JUNK PROGRAM

It's like a virus you didn't even know was installed, lurking in the background of your mind, draining energy, slowing you down, corrupting files you don't even remember creating. Fear is that junk program. It's buried deep in your mental code, feeding off every thought, shadowing every action, running so silently you mistake its grinding noise for your own thinking.

Fear was meant to be a safety program—a warning when you're walking too close to the edge or an instinctual jump back when danger lurks. But somewhere along the line, it infected every part of the system. It slipped from the background into the forefront, convincing you that *everything* in life is a threat, that every decision has to be cautious, defensive, small. And we've bought into it. We live as if it's normal to run life from a fear-based operating system, while our potential is dragged down to its knees.

Let's be clear: if humanity was designed to evolve, fear wasn't supposed to lead the way. And yet, look at the world we've built. Societies rise and fall under the same mantra of scarcity, fighting for dominance, conquest, power plays. The game hasn't changed since the

Roman era; it's just dressed in modern clothes. Empires still rise and fall. We're still chasing power. We're still afraid someone's coming to take what's "ours." The whole system is rotten with the same mind virus that's had us locked in cycles of lack and control, one scared human after another scrambling to protect their corner of a reality they barely control.

Power and Fear: A Brutal Combination

Power and fear are a brutal combination, the twin architects of our collective reality. We've used them to shape entire civilizations, building systems of control to keep our fears at bay. But when power is rooted in fear, it's a shaky foundation. It drives a need for dominance, for manipulation, for the hoarding of resources and influence. We've created systems that thrive on lack, pitting people against one another in a race for survival. We're not evolving; we're stuck on repeat.

We've outgrown this. Fear, unchecked, is a drag on humanity's evolution. It's a junk program that poisons everything it touches. And if we want to become truly humane, it's time we learned to put fear back in its place—as a tool, not a tyrant. You don't need to eliminate fear; you need to reprogram it, to put it in an advisory role, assisting in the background where it belongs. You need higher intelligence, evolved emotions, and a deep commitment to living with intent, stepping up to become the one in command.

The Absurdity of the Fear-Driven Life

Let's call it like it is: it's *stupid* to keep thinking this way. It's absurd to assume that this anxious, fear-driven loop is our highest potential. Why is humanity still caged by the same old patterns, the same tired mentality? It's not only unintelligent; it's self-destructive. And yet, we've made it the baseline.

Demonizing the ego, treating it like a monster that needs to be tamed instead of the engine that can drive us forward—what sense does that make? Fear will tell you to play it safe, to manage the small problems without asking better questions, to believe that you're flawed at the core. This mindset of self-sabotage, this endless loop of managing fears and perceived failures, is not evolution. It's barely survival.

Let's be real. Feeding your mind with garbage—constant thoughts of inadequacy, worry, lack—is just as destructive as feeding your body a diet of toxins. You don't heal a system by drowning it in more of what caused the illness to begin with. Yet most of us let fear sit at the helm, feeding it, nursing it, letting it run riot through our thoughts and beliefs. What does that produce? More garbage, more junk code, more stagnation.

The Victimhood Trap: The Doorway to the Mind Virus

The fear-driven mind has one main message: you're a victim of your life. It'll convince you that everything that happens to you is out of your control, that the cards were dealt long before you came to the table. But here's the truth: as a soul, you chose this life. You chose the challenges, the experiences, the exact conditions of your existence. Why? Because there's something in this life for you to learn, to master. But fear wants to keep you from that realization. It wants you to play small, stay guarded, repeat the same mistakes, run the same cycles.

When you buy into the lie of victimhood, you open the door to the mind virus. You become a pawn to your own life, managing small grievances instead of expanding into the creator you were designed to be. Fear's main trick is to make you believe you're surviving when in reality, you're only managing symptoms, haunted by a system you could be rewriting.

The Upgrade: Introducing Intelligent Thinking

Upgrading your operating system means introducing a new paradigm: intelligent thinking. It means realizing that you have the power to choose how you process information, to align your decisions with higher intelligence, not with base survival instincts. You can't heal the mind by feeding it more fear-based thoughts, just like you can't heal a body on a diet of processed food. Holistic, nourishing thoughts are the only way forward—clear, empowering beliefs that build you up instead of tearing you down.

Consider the current state of your mind like the American diet—laced with additives, sugar, and chemicals that erode the body's natural function. Fear does the same to the mind, breaking down emotional, spiritual, and mental health, corrupting your operating system with every cycle of insecurity, comparison, and lack. But the solution isn't to run from fear or deny its existence; the solution is to put it in its place.

Fear can exist, but it must be guided, given parameters, told when to show up and when to step back. This upgrade isn't about fighting or eliminating fear. It's about using it as a minor program within a much larger, much more powerful system. You're not here to run from your reality, to keep playing small. You're here to take command of your mind, to program it consciously, to eliminate the junk data of victimhood and replace it with beliefs that elevate, expand, and empower.

Claiming Your Role as Creator, Not Victim

The endgame here is evolution—not just as a means of surviving but as a path to mastery. If fear has been your default awareness, this is the point where you move beyond it, where you take full responsibility for your life and actions. To step into the role of creator is to live with full presence and purpose, to become the one who decides how every facet of your mind operates. You become the coder, rewriting your mental landscape with clarity, awareness, and command.

With this upgrade, you put yourself back in the driver's seat. No more managing symptoms, no more running loops, no more mental stagnation. Instead, you live with purpose, with intelligence, free from the dead weight of the mind virus. This is evolution: the courage to rise above fear, to think with purpose, to live with intent. The path forward is clear—step into your own power, rewrite the program, and claim your place as the architect of your reality.

11

COMMANDING FEAR

Fear is a nag. It's the whiny, persistent voice that shows up when you're reaching for more, gripping at the edges of your dreams and possibilities, telling you that danger is lurking in every shadow. But let's be real: fear is not the appropriate response to every new thing in your life. When you're focused on creating your reality—stepping into the unknown and meeting parts of yourself you haven't met yet—fear is inevitable, yes, but it doesn't need to lead the way. You are not here to be managed by fear. You are here to command it.

Evolution is not some monstrous threat on the horizon; it's an invitation, a warm and steady light guiding you into your potential. If the universe handed you the magic you seek, would you scream and run, or would you open your hands and welcome it? Fear isn't the way you'd react to a friend, especially one who's offering you an expanded reality, a life more fully aligned with your truth and purpose. And if you know who you are—if you're certain of the intelligence and support that the universe has woven around you—then fear becomes irrelevant, a reaction for those who live without the awareness of their own power.

It's time to recognize this: fear is designed to fuel your evolution, not to hold you back. But instead of shutting it out or denying it, you offer it something better, something accurate. You offer it the truth. This isn't about pretending fear doesn't exist or waging a constant war against it. It's about commanding fear, stepping into a place of certainty, and using fear as a tool rather than a master. Because to step into your fullest potential, you don't need less fear—you need more truth.

The Reality of Fear: The Mental Virus

Fear starts in the mind. It feeds on illusion, taking innocent "what ifs" and spinning them into full-scale catastrophes. Fear's entire power lies in its ability to imagine things that haven't happened and may never happen. It whispers that if you step up, show yourself, create something new, you'll be hurt, embarrassed, or worse. And we believe it. The mind turns fear into an obsessive narrative, an all-consuming loop that distorts reality and paralyzes our potential.

Most of us have been conditioned to respect fear, even cater to it. We make excuses for our inaction and chalk it up to "being safe." But safety is just the polite name we give fear when we want to keep it in charge. Look at humanity's history—empires rose and fell, not because of bravery or vision, but because fear wormed its way into the foundations. Nations, relationships, businesses, all crumble under the weight of fear, as people pull back, protect, and distrust each other. Power and fear together have shaped most of our reality, creating cycles of violence, dominance, and self-preservation. We've been here, repeating the same patterns for millennia.

Recognizing the Real Enemy: Fear's Role in Holding You Back

Fear's real trick is that it convinces you to guard against everything, to focus on survival instead of creation. It makes you doubt your power, second-guess your intuition, and assume that freedom, success, and joy come with unbearable risks. Fear is a junk program because it clogs up your mind, sapping energy from every part of your system. Instead of moving toward what you want, you're left managing an endless list of "what ifs," convinced you're safer doing nothing.

It's time to make a choice: command fear, or let it command you. Because the truth is, fear will always show up where growth is possible. Want to start a new project? Fear tells you it will fail. Ready to leave a toxic relationship? Fear paints a picture of loneliness. Dreaming of changing your entire life? Fear warns that you'll lose what little security you have.

Here's the reality—anything worth doing will evoke some fear. Commanding fear means acknowledging it, even respecting its message, but making a choice *in spite* of it.

Shutting Down the Nagging Voice with Command and Clarity

Fear loves to cling to every unknown, especially when you're close to a breakthrough. It can show up like static, fuzzing up the signal, bringing in doubts, hesitation, and the illusion of danger where there is none. This is the moment to step in with authority. If fear is nagging, then your mind needs clear, direct commands to reprogram that noise. Let's be clear: this is not a suggestion; this is how you lead your mind.

Start with this: *"Fear is not an appropriate response."* Say it, own it, make it a mantra that rings through your mental corridors. When you're stepping into the unknown, it's not fear that should fill the space. It's clarity, conviction, focus. Commanding fear is not about dismissing it; it's about directing it, telling it where it belongs. You relegate it to its designated role, which is to heighten your senses, not your doubts. The choice command is this: *I choose clarity over confusion. I choose creation over fear.* Repeat it, embed it, believe it.

Meeting Fear with Accurate Thinking

Fear thrives on inaccurate thinking, on worst-case scenarios that haven't happened and likely never will. So, if fear is going to show up, the answer isn't avoidance—it's accuracy. What are you actually dealing with? Are you truly in danger, or is fear trying to trick you into thinking the unknown is a threat? If you're stepping into a new role, creating something, leaving behind what no longer serves you, fear will try to cloak that path in shadows. It will point out everything that could go wrong, everything that might fail, everyone who could judge. But here's the truth: fear cannot predict the future, and it cannot define your worth.

When fear rises, meet it with accuracy. *What exactly am I afraid of?* Break it down until there's nowhere left for fear to hide. Is there anything you can't handle? Can fear point to any real evidence that this unknown is a danger? In most cases, fear's accusations dissolve under the light of clear thinking, revealing it for what it is—a conditioned response that doesn't belong here.

Neuroplasticity and Cognitive Flexibility: Rewiring the Ego

Neuroplasticity is the brain's remarkable ability to reorganize itself by forming new neural connections. It is the foundation for learning, memory, and adaptation. The New Ego Theory leverages neuroplasticity to rewire the ego's processing system, allowing for deep, lasting transformation.

Each time you issue a choice command, you're not just shifting your mindset temporarily—you're actively rewiring your brain. Neuroplasticity allows the ego to adapt, creating new pathways that align with your higher self, rather than reinforcing old patterns of fear, doubt, or limitation.

- Cognitive Flexibility: This adaptability is known as cognitive flexibility—the ability to switch between different thought processes or perspectives. By using choice commands, you increase the ego's cognitive flexibility, enabling it to process new information in a way that aligns with your desired outcomes.

The beauty of this process is that it is self-directed. You are not at the mercy of your past programming or external circumstances. Instead, you have the power to consciously choose how your brain rewires itself through the ego's data processing system.

• Example of Neuroplasticity in Action: If you've always viewed failure as something negative, your ego has likely been wired to avoid risks or challenges that might result in failure. But through choice commands like "I choose to embrace failure as part of growth," you start to rewire your ego's processing system. Over time, your brain will form new connections that associate failure with learning and growth, making you more resilient and open to challenges.

Practical Tools for Commanding Fear

1. Choice Commands: Fear is loud, and it loves to repeat itself. To drown out fear, you need to speak with authority over your mind. This is where choice commands come in—simple, powerful statements that remind you who's in control. Examples?

"I choose to relate to states of power and raw energy in my system as a beautiful truth"

"I choose to utilize my power."

"I choose to define what joy feels like in my body.

"I choose to define what freedom feels like in my body."

Choice commands are orders to your system, declarations that make fear's grip loosen. Start your day with them. Use them before stepping into anything new or intimidating. Speak them out loud when fear tries to creep in, and watch your mind recalibrate.

2. Dispel the Illusion: Fear lives off of the unknown, the hypothetical, the worst-case scenario. Get specific. What exactly are you afraid will happen? Write it down, make it tangible. Then question it: how likely is it? What's the worst that could actually happen, and could you handle that? Fear loses power the moment you expose it to the light of logic.

3. Repetition of the Ten Dimensions Command Sequence: Reinforce your mental operating system by running the DivineOS sequence daily. Speed, Storage, Story, Senses, Security, Soul, Subconscious, Systems, Seventh Sense, Sphere—each layer serves to keep fear in its place, reminding you of your vast potential beyond fear's cage. Use it as your grounding tool, a reminder of the power within every level of your consciousness.

4. Take Physical Action Against Fear: Fear often dissipates the moment you move into action. Want to start a business? Take the first step, no matter how small. Want to leave a toxic environment? Begin planning your exit today. Action pulls you out of your mind and into reality, proving that fear's projections are just illusions. It's hard for fear to control a mind that's focused on tangible progress.

Commanding Fear: A Lifelong Practice

Fear will continue to shape-shift; the more you evolve, the more it adapts. You may tackle fear in one area only for it to pop up in another. As you get more comfortable taking risks, fear will show up in new ways, like a chameleon in your mind. But commanding fear is a lifelong practice, a commitment to recognizing its tricks and choosing to rise above them. Don't expect to completely eradicate fear—that's not the goal. Instead, relegate it to its rightful place.

It's a lot like training a muscle. The more you practice choice commands, the more your mind responds to them automatically. The more you confront fear with action, the less control it has over you. And as you build that muscle, you reclaim parts of yourself that were once locked in fear's grasp. This is the process of mastery.

Understanding Fear in Body and Mind

It's crucial to distinguish between mind-fear and body-fear. The body responds naturally to danger: a car speeding toward you, a fall, physical harm. That's instinct, a survival mechanism hardwired to keep you alive. But fear in the mind? That's an invention, an illusion of control meant to prevent imagined harm. The body moves out of instinct, but the mind latches onto illusions. Commanding fear requires you to know the difference.

When you're safe in your environment, yet gripped by anxiety about your future, failure, or judgment, that's the fear running the show.

12

THE 10 DIMENSIONS OF AWARENESS: A FRAMEWORK FOR ORGANIZING THE EGO

The **10 Dimensions of Awareness** serve as a foundational framework, giving structure to the ego's processing. Imagine each dimension as a checkpoint or filter that refines your perception of reality, enabling the ego to function with high precision. By integrating this framework, you provide your ego with a guided pathway for interpreting experiences, aligning it with both your individual purpose and universal connection.

The sequence of the 10 Dimensions is as follows:

1. **Speed**: Governs the rate at which data enters your awareness.
   - *"I choose to regulate the speed of incoming information, allowing only what serves my highest focus."*
2. **Storage**: Decides what to retain in your awareness, storing only what aligns with growth.
   - *"I choose to store only the empowering insights that support my journey."*
3. **Story**: Crafts the narrative around experiences. The ego frames each event to reflect truth, not limitation.

- *"I choose to create a story of courage, truth, and potential."*
4. **Senses**: Uses physical and intuitive senses to filter data points, tuning into genuine intuition.
   - *"I choose to trust my senses, discerning truth from distraction."*
5. **Security**: Maintains a sense of safety rooted in reality, not fear-based assumptions.
   - *"I choose to ground myself in true security, filtering out illusory fears."*
6. **Soul**: Aligns with the purpose of your soul, fact-checking experiences against your deeper truth.
   - *"I choose to act in alignment with my soul's vision."*
7. **Subconscious**: Recognizes and integrates subconscious patterns, aligning them with conscious intentions.
   - *"I choose to release subconscious programs that no longer serve me."*
8. **Systems**: Understands societal influences, allowing you to choose alignment with personal values over conformity.
   - *"I choose to engage with systems that resonate with my truth."*
9. **Seventh Sense**: Accesses a heightened level of awareness, tuning into the higher truth beyond surface appearances.
   - *"I choose to connect with my seventh sense, perceiving truth beyond the visible."*
10. **Sphere**: Grounds the self as a unique yet interconnected whole, holding the duality of individuality within universal oneness.
    - *"I choose to ground myself in my complete self, connected to all yet fully me."*

Each choice command aligns the ego within a specific dimension, transforming it from a reactive filter into a tool of precision and clarity.

Putting the Framework into Practice

Let's consider a practical example: you're about to launch a new project, but self-doubt and fear of failure begin to cloud your mind. Here's how you would organize the ego with choice commands and the 10 Dimensions to reframe your experience:

1. **Speed**: *"I choose to regulate the speed of my thoughts, focusing only on productive information."*
2. **Storage**: *"I choose to store only the empowering insights that support my vision."*
3. **Story**: *"I choose to create a story of courage and commitment in this endeavor."*
4. **Senses**: *"I choose to trust my senses, discerning truth from distraction."*
5. **Security**: *"I choose true security, releasing fears that do not serve me."*
6. **Soul**: *"I choose to align with my soul's purpose in this work."*
7. **Subconscious**: *"I choose to release outdated beliefs about judgment and failure."*
8. **Systems**: *"I choose values that resonate with my truth, not societal expectations."*
9. **Seventh Sense**: *"I choose to view this project with a heightened awareness of my potential."*
10. **Sphere**: *"I choose to ground in my complete self, connected to all yet uniquely me."*

By running your experience through these 10 Dimensions, the ego processes information accurately, grounded in your higher intentions. It no longer clings to fears or doubts; it aligns with the purpose of your creation.

A Revolutionary Perspective: The Ego as a Bridge Between Self and Universal Consciousness

This approach to organizing the ego is nothing short of revolutionary. By using choice commands and the 10 Dimensions, you transform the ego from a reactive filter into a clear conduit between your individual self and universal awareness. This method acknowledges the ego's value as a processor, not something to eliminate but to refine. Organized properly, the ego aligns with your divine will, helping you to build a life that reflects your highest purpose.

When the ego is organized, it no longer needs to control, defend, or compete. It becomes a grounding tool, bridging individuality and unity, fact-checking reality without distortion. Through choice commands, you consciously direct this bridge, aligning your singular consciousness with universal flow.

Living from an Organized Ego: The Foundation of Clear Creation

An organized ego creates a profound shift in every area of life. No longer bound by societal programming or fear-based thinking, you begin to engage with reality from a place of clarity, grounded in your true self. The ego, aligned with both your individuality and universal connection, becomes the foundation of your highest expression. You're free to build, create, and evolve without the weight of distortion, empowered to live a life that mirrors your true value and purpose.

Organizing the ego is more than a daily practice; it's the foundation of The New Ego Theory. It redefines the ego as a powerful, precise tool that enables you to walk the path of alignment with confidence, clarity, and divine will. Through this framework, the ego no longer distorts but illuminates, creating a bridge between your singular experience and the infinite potential of universal consciousness.

PART IV
THE MIND MATRIX

13

THE SINGULAR MATRIX AND THE LIFE FIELD

Imagine a world where every individual walks through life in a self-contained, invisible matrix, a sphere uniquely constructed for each person. This *singular matrix* is the architecture of your reality, one that interacts constantly with the collective matrix surrounding it. Picture yourself as a sphere within a larger sphere; the outer field presses upon your inner field, challenging and shaping it. This pressure is neither incidental nor trivial; it's the necessary catalyst for your evolution.

In this dynamic relationship between your singular matrix and the collective matrix, your task isn't to resist the pressure but to strengthen your own inner sphere—to reinforce the beliefs, values, and operating systems that support your personal growth. Just as the dense, compact center of a star can withstand immense gravitational forces, the resilience of your inner matrix determines how you handle life's pressures.

The Singular Matrix: Your Life Field

In this perspective, your singular matrix is known as the *life field*. This life field isn't just a concept; it's a living awareness that holds your purpose, intentions, and everything you create. It's your personal universe, reflecting both who you are and who you are becoming. When you see life this way, every experience, every person, and every challenge that enters your field has meaning. Life is no longer something happening to you but something happening *through* you, constantly shaping and refining your personal matrix.

But how do you strengthen this singular matrix to ensure it serves your highest growth? It begins with self-support and wisdom. Self-support means you cultivate the inner resilience to handle whatever arises. You become your own foundation, no longer waiting for external validation or approval to define your reality. Wisdom, meanwhile, transforms knowledge into embodied understanding, teaching you to discern between truth and illusion in every experience.

The Constructive Pressure of the Collective Matrix

Much like tectonic plates pressing against each other to form mountains, the interaction between your singular matrix and the collective matrix creates the catalyst for growth. This pressure isn't inherently negative. Rather, it exists to push you toward expansion and self-clarity. The beliefs, norms, and energies of the collective will inevitably press into your field, and your job is to decide what enters and what does not, thereby strengthening your core.

Many of us, instead of strengthening our singular matrix, find ourselves bending under the collective matrix's influence, absorbing societal fears, expectations, and definitions of success. Imagine trying to create something original but finding yourself weighed down by inherited fears, borrowed beliefs, and distractions that dilute your own sense of purpose. This is what happens when we don't actively strengthen our singular matrix. The outer pressure consumes us rather than catalyzing our growth.

The Life Field in Action: Becoming the Creator of Your Experience

In practical terms, living from the perspective of the life field is about owning every experience that enters your sphere. If you're feeling insecure about a new job, your life field has invited this challenge to strengthen your resilience, not weaken it. Instead of seeking answers externally, you ask: *What do I already know? What inner resources can I draw upon?*

To illustrate, consider this example. Let's say you feel overwhelmed by a financial challenge. Instead of seeking a quick solution or waiting for external help, you center yourself within your life field and remind yourself that you have the power to create and attract resources. You begin by using choice commands, affirming the direction of your energy and thoughts:

- *"I choose to be resourceful."*
- *"I choose to see abundance within my reach."*
- *"I choose to release fear around money and trust in my ability to create wealth."*

Each of these commands is a directive to your life field, fortifying your matrix against external pressures and aligning your focus with your chosen reality.

Intuition and Desire within the Life Field

Operating within the life field transforms your relationship with intuition. When you're out of alignment, intuition feels like an endless series of guesses, a compass without true north. You may ask questions like, *Should I pursue this career path? Is this relationship right for me?*

Such questions reveal doubt, which often arises from fear of making the "wrong" choice.

In the life field, however, intuition merges with desire, becoming a seamless expression of your will. The need to seek direction dissipates because you are no longer looking for answers outside yourself. The life field itself responds to your intentions, and external circumstances arise to support your vision. It's like having a conversation with life where both you and the life field speak in the same language, sharing a mutual understanding.

This isn't some passive waiting for signs. It's a deliberate act of creation, an ongoing conversation with the universe in which you ask, listen, and the life field responds. If you desire something—a successful career, a loving relationship, financial freedom—that desire isn't a random wish. It's an invitation from you to your life field to create and experience what is already part of your potential.

Strengthening the Singular Matrix: Foundations and Fundamentals

A strong relationship with your life field requires solid foundations and fundamentals—core beliefs, values, and perspectives that you return to regularly. These principles act as stabilizing pillars within your matrix, grounding you in self-support and wisdom. They provide a reliable reference point, so when the collective matrix pressures you to conform or compromise, you know where you stand.

Some foundational beliefs to cultivate include:

• *Belief in Your Power to Create*: This is the understanding that everything you experience is an extension of your will and focus.

• *Self-Support*: Develop the ability to ground yourself emotionally, mentally, and spiritually. This is the antidote to victimhood. When you support yourself, you don't need to depend on others for validation.

- *Wisdom over Knowledge*: Wisdom transforms knowledge into lived experience. When you operate from wisdom, you don't need external proof to affirm your direction.

These foundations give your singular matrix the strength to withstand the pressures of the collective matrix without collapsing.

Living as the Life Field: The End of Seeking

The life field perspective marks the end of seeking. Instead of searching outside yourself for answers, validations, or signs, you recognize that life itself is speaking to you, guiding you, and mirroring your intentions. You become, in essence, your own prophecy. The external world shifts from a place of uncertainty to a reflection of your inner alignment.

Consider this: every synchronicity, every "coincidence," every unexpected turn of events is a dialogue with your life field. When you observe this with the understanding that *you* are the one creating the experience, the matrix strengthens. It becomes a feedback loop of empowerment, where you set an intention, witness life respond, and then affirm that response by grounding further in your reality.

Strengthening the Life Field with Choice Commands

The practice of choice commands is central to organizing and fortifying your life field. Each command begins with "I choose," a statement that asserts your authority over your reality. It's not about hoping for change or wishing for luck; it's about deciding. Every time you issue a choice command, you are building your matrix, aligning it with your highest potential and aligning the singular matrix with the broader life field.

Sample choice commands to strengthen your life field:

- *"I choose to cultivate clarity in all my interactions."*

- *"I choose to see every experience as an opportunity for growth."*
- *"I choose to recognize and strengthen the foundation of my life field."*

Through choice commands, you are not only organizing the ego but also embedding your intentions in every layer of the matrix, reinforcing the architecture of your singular life field and aligning it with the collective field from a place of strength rather than reactivity.

Embracing the Life Field: Moving Beyond the Illusion of Separation

The singular matrix within the collective matrix is a concept that, once understood, can transform your experience of reality. You're no longer searching, waiting, or hoping. Instead, you're walking through life with the awareness that every challenge and every joy is a reflection of your inner alignment, an invitation to strengthen your life field further.

When you live within the life field, you no longer see life as something that happens to you; you see it as something that happens *through* you. And as you strengthen your singular matrix, your life becomes a symphony of creation—a beautiful, intricate, and evolving sphere of growth, aligned with your soul and the universal consciousness.

Your journey isn't about escaping the pressure of the external; it's about using it as a catalyst to forge your own singular matrix into something resilient, beautiful, and uniquely yours. Welcome to the path of living from the life field. Here, you are not just a part of reality; you are its creator.

14

THE PATH OF POLARITY AND CHOICE

Choice: the first and final freedom. It's the axis upon which your reality spins, the one weapon in your arsenal against despair, fear, and the heaviness of existence. In every moment, you stand at a gateway—a portal that beckons you to step through. One side opens to limitation, to low vibrations, to the familiar gray tones of survival. The other side offers clarity, expansion, and the wild landscapes of higher realms.

In these higher realms, you don't simply survive; you create. You don't merely react; you respond. This is the life field of polarity, where you're invited to explore both ends of the spectrum but, through awareness, make a conscious choice. It's a path lined with powerful, undeniable truths and a calling that you may feel deep in your bones—a call to move beyond the limitations of a human conditioned to fear.

A Life of Polarity: The Field of Choice

From birth, you're thrust into a world steeped in duality. Light and dark, love and hate, joy and suffering—polarity is the essence of human experience. But here's the secret that escapes most: polarity is not a prison but a spectrum. The more aware you become, the more you realize that each experience, even the painful, exists as a choice. You can lean toward one side or the other, hold your suffering close or open yourself to transformation.

Think back to your lowest moments, those times when life felt like an inescapable hell, a maze of suffering and frustration. We all have them. I remember a time in my life that felt so consuming it turned my body into a map of aches and exhaustion, as if my cells themselves were screaming out for release. Days would end with a bone-deep ache, an exhaustion that wasn't just physical but spiritual. I existed in a field of density, fighting shadows I couldn't see, unsure if light even existed on the other side.

What kept me going wasn't some external promise of salvation. It was a whisper from somewhere deep within—a spark that knew this wasn't the end of my story. That even in this dense, almost suffocating field, I had a choice. And that's the truth at the core of this matrix: you are never without choice. It may seem small, almost inconsequential, but it is there, alive and potent. In every moment, you can choose to tilt toward growth, toward freedom.

The Paradox of Polarity: Embracing the Shadow and Light

Polarity is not an invitation to deny one side in favor of the other. This path isn't about rejecting darkness to cling to light, nor about fleeing struggle to chase endless peace. Polarity is the dance between both, a field where each emotion, each thought, serves a purpose. You are the paradox itself, embodying both heaven and hell, joy and sorrow, strength and vulnerability. It is in acknowledging the totality of your experience that you find freedom—not through avoidance, but through full awareness and choice.

We are all coded with a unique set of divine aspects that call us to different experiences. Maybe you're here to embody resilience, to be someone who stands strong even when others would crumble. Or perhaps you're meant to be a mirror, reflecting love even in spaces steeped in fear. Each of us is designed to live in polarity while ultimately choosing the path that serves our highest vision. Your soul didn't come here to escape duality but to use it as fuel for transformation.

The Heavy Cost of Apathy

The lowest frequency on this path isn't suffering; it's apathy. When you're in pain, at least you're feeling something, moving through something. Apathy, however, is the absence of all movement, the numbing of the soul. It's the resignation that comes from believing you're powerless, from abandoning the path of choice. Apathy isn't just a surrender; it's a surrender to nothingness, a refusal to live at all.

When you choose to rise from apathy, you step back into your role as creator. You reclaim the ability to choose joy over despair, growth over stagnation, self-leadership over helplessness. This is not about pretending that suffering isn't real or glossing over the complexity of life. It's about recognizing that even when faced with darkness, you possess the power to turn toward light.

Living from the Higher Realms

When you operate from a place of conscious choice, you're no longer tossed around by external forces. You become the eye of the storm—a still point from which life unfolds, but not by chance or fate. Every experience, even those that seem like setbacks, becomes fuel for your evolution. And the more you practice, the more you find yourself existing within higher vibrational states, moving fluidly through the density of polarity and choosing to live from love, joy, and creation.

Imagine life as a river with two banks: one of suffering and the other of liberation. Most people drift passively, caught in the current, reacting to whichever side pulls them strongest. But when you live from the higher realms, you are not in the current. You're the one steering, deliberately choosing which shore to land upon. This doesn't mean you never experience challenges, but rather that you approach each one with a deep inner knowledge that you have chosen to meet it.

The Power of Choice as Divine Liberation

If every human could understand one thing, it would be this: you are not powerless. The weight of your life is not determined by fate, nor are you bound by a predefined destiny. You are a creator, living in a matrix of choices that shape your reality. Each day offers countless opportunities to rise, to choose again, to step out of the shadows and into the light.

It's tempting to search outside yourself for deliverance, to look for answers in teachings, signs, and prophecies. But true liberation doesn't come from external sources. It comes from the courage to choose, moment after moment, to live as the architect of your experience.

If life presents a challenge, you choose how to see it, how to move through it, and ultimately, what it will mean to you. When you choose to view every moment as an opportunity for growth, even pain becomes a tool, a mirror that reflects your strength back to you.

Moving Beyond Duality: Toward Singular States of Creation

At the highest level of this path, you access what's known as singular states of creation—realms of being where duality dissolves. These are states where love, joy, peace, and clarity are constant, unshaken by the shifting landscapes of life. This is not to say that you escape polarity entirely, but that you experience it differently. You are no longer pulled between extremes, no longer reactive to every push and pull of the external world.

In a singular state of creation, you exist in unity. Your desires, intuition, and actions align seamlessly, so you don't have to search or strive. You simply are. Imagine love as a steady hum, an ever-present frequency. That's what it's like to live in a singular state: unwavering, vibrant, alive.

Stepping Through the Portal

The path of polarity and choice is a lifelong journey. It's a rebellion against passivity, a stand against the stories that have kept humanity bound in fear and density for millennia. When you walk this path, you're not just choosing for yourself. You're carving a new way forward for others, showing them that liberation is not an abstract concept but a living, breathing reality.

You're the one who decides how high you rise. You're the one who chooses whether to dwell in shadow or light. And each day, you reinforce that choice with every thought, every word, every action. This is the path of the soul-led life, the path of radical responsibility and breathtaking freedom. Step forward. Choose. Let every moment be a portal to the reality you desire.

15

THE UPGRADE

In the complexity of our daily lives, filled with continuous input, rapid responses, and relentless mental chatter, the concept of upgrading our mind's operating system is no longer an abstract luxury—it's a necessity. This upgrade is more than a personal improvement strategy; it's a structured elevation, an evolution of how we interpret reality, manage emotional turbulence, and ultimately, lead ourselves through life's polarity with clarity and resilience.

The Upgrade: A Pathway to Clarity and Resilience

Our minds, like a well-architected operating system, are constantly processing, storing, and recalling information. However, in a world flooded with data and driven by both internal and external demands, most of us are functioning on a reactive, outdated system—one that isn't aligned with the fast-paced, high-information environment we exist in today. The **10 Dimensions of Awareness** are tools that, when understood and integrated, allow us to harness the mind's full capacity with precision and intent.

The upgrade begins with awareness of these dimensions, each representing a key component in our cognitive and emotional processing, each offering a specific function to help us address and transform incoming information, emotions, and experience. By understanding these, we gain not only functionality but a profound freedom from states of overwhelm and scattered focus.

Why We Need the Upgrade: The Problem with Our Default Settings

Our default cognitive system is highly influenced by the environment, often bogged down by stories and unchecked assumptions formed through past experiences, inherited beliefs, and reactive emotions. This mental framework is not equipped to filter and prioritize data at the speed required for true, empowered choice. Studies on cognitive overload confirm that our minds have limited processing capacity, which, when exceeded, can lead to decision fatigue, emotional burnout, and loss of focus where the 10 Dimensions come into play, allowing us to "clear the clutter" of mental processing, prioritize what matters, and let go of what doesn't.

Living in the Upgrade: Moving Beyond Reaction to Creation

In practical terms, the upgrade brings you back into the driver's seat of your life. Instead of being yanked around by circumstance, you become the designer of your responses, your narrative, and ultimately, your experience. Consider the daily stresses of modern life: your mind is bombarded with decisions and demands, each adding to the cognitive load that wears down clarity and resilience. Studies indicate that by proactively managing the flow of incoming data—organizing it, simplifying it, and filtering unnecessary clutter—we improve focus and decision-making ability while reducing stress .

With this upgrade, you start each day from a place of centered awareness, choosing the data that supports you and filtering out what distracts or detracts. You don't reactively consume information; you selectively engage. You replace anxiety about keeping up with the pace of life with the confidence of self-command.

The Emotional Freedom of Living in the Upgrade

Imagine the freedom of not being tied to every random thought or emotional reaction. When you live in the upgraded system, you aren't bound by outdated narratives. Instead, you experience emotions as guides, sensing them deeply yet remaining undistracted by emotional turbulence. You interact with feelings like indicators on a dashboard, honoring each as relevant but not allowing any to take control.

Think of it as moving from surviving the chaos of life to thriving within it. Life continues to happen around you, but in your upgraded mind, you're not drained by its demands. Your energy is channeled toward what resonates with your purpose, your joy, and your highest growth. This shift alone liberates countless hours spent in mental spirals, freeing you to live with more presence and purpose.

The Path Forward: Choosing the Upgrade Daily

This upgrade isn't a one-time decision; it's a daily practice of alignment and choice. Every moment becomes an opportunity to reaffirm your chosen state, to return to clarity, and to engage with life from a place of intentionality. This way, the 10 Dimensions become integrated into your daily existence. You no longer view them as steps to be remembered; they are the way you operate, effortlessly, as you navigate life.

The upgrade moves you beyond living reactively, creating a life led by proactive choice and empowered awareness. It's the process of evolving from a scattered mind bound by limitation to an organized, purposeful one that experiences life as a harmonious flow. It's not just about thinking differently; it's about living in a way that reflects your truest potential.

As you embody the upgraded system, you find yourself experiencing reality from an elevated perspective—a life field where you are no longer tossed by the waves but stand calmly, shaping them with intentional command. This is the power of living in alignment with the 10 Dimensions. This is the freedom of the upgrade.

16

THE EGO AS A CATALYST FOR EVOLUTION

At its core, The New Ego Theory is about transformation. But this transformation extends beyond the individual—it has the potential to shape humanity's collective evolution. When we consciously align our ego with divine potential, we open the door to a new era of spiritual awakening and personal empowerment.

• Bridging the Divine and the Human: The ego, in its role as a data processor, serves as the bridge between divine energy and human action. It is the translator of divine intention into tangible results. When aligned with our higher consciousness, the ego becomes the vehicle through which our divine potential is expressed in the physical world.

  ◦ Example: Think of the ego as a lens. When it is clouded by fear, doubt, and limiting beliefs, our divine light is obscured, and our actions are misaligned with our true purpose. But when the ego is reprogrammed and clarified through intentional choice, that lens becomes clear, allowing divine light to shine through, guiding our actions with precision and purpose.

• Accelerating Collective Evolution: The ripple effect of individual transformation cannot be understated. As more people begin to apply the principles of The New Ego Theory, we will see a shift in collective consciousness. The ego, once viewed as a source of separation, becomes a tool for unity, collaboration, and collective growth.

◦ Example: When individuals reprogram their ego to align with compassion, abundance, and empowerment, those shifts are reflected in their interactions with others. Imagine a world where communities consciously practice ego reprogramming, fostering environments of collaboration, creativity, and love. The result is a collective awakening, where the ego no longer divides but unites us in our shared pursuit of spiritual and personal evolution.

Ethical Responsibility and the Future of The New Ego Theory

With great power comes great responsibility. The ability to consciously reprogram the ego carries with it ethical implications. As we move into the future, practitioners of The New Ego Theory must approach this work with integrity, using it to uplift and empower, rather than manipulate or control.

• Empowerment, Not Manipulation: The tools of ego reprogramming should always be used to align individuals with their highest potential. In the wrong hands, these techniques could be used to influence or control others. It is essential that we use these tools responsibly, always seeking to empower and uplift those around us.

• Collective Responsibility: As we embrace The New Ego Theory on a larger scale, we must also consider the broader societal and environmental impacts of our choices. When we reprogram our ego to align with divine potential, we are not just acting for ourselves—we are acting on behalf of the collective consciousness.

◦ Example: Imagine leaders, educators, and healers practicing the new ego theory within DivineOS, using these tools to create positive change in their communities. The result is a ripple effect that spreads through society, transforming not just individual lives but entire systems and structures.

As we come to the conclusion of this journey through The New Ego Theory, it's important to reflect on the transformation we've set in motion. The ego, once viewed through the lens of limitation and conflict, has been redefined as a dynamic tool for conscious evolution. We've explored its capacity to act as a data processing center, adapting to intentional input and serving as the bridge between our human experiences and our divine potential.

In this final part, we will summarize the most important aspects of the theory, emphasizing how the ego, when integrated into the DivineOS framework, becomes not only a tool for personal growth but also a catalyst for our spiritual and collective evolution.

Included in this book are 50 Choice Command Sequences. For a comprehensive experience, the full DivineOS upgrade features 122 sequences, offered as part of our client services.

17

BEYOND DEFAULT: ACTIVATING DIVINEOS FOR CONSCIOUS EVOLUTION

This is where your journey with the DivineOS sequence becomes an actionable, transformative process—a pattern interrupt for the mind. Picture the upgrade as an intentional re-coding, a recalibration that allows you to move beyond the mind's default settings and into a space where choice, clarity, and elevated states of being are your natural operating mode. This tool isn't just a way to clear cluttered thoughts; it's a direct line to creating a reality led by empowered choices, where every experience becomes an invitation to command your awareness and direct your focus toward your highest purpose.

How to Use the Upgrade

The DivineOS sequence + Choice commands operates as a simple yet profound tool: a pattern interrupt that steps in to reorganize, refocus, and elevate your thought process whenever you encounter stress, looping thoughts, or negative emotional states. When you find yourself in a moment of doubt, fear, or mental chaos, the sequence is there to provide an alternative—a reset back to conscious awareness. It shifts you from reactive thinking to deliberate choice, from a state of anxious reaction to a state of mindful, elevated action.

Using it is straightforward. The sequence is:

- **Speed, Storage, Story, Senses, Security, Soul, Subconscious, System, Seventh Sense, Sphere**

Repeat it. Say it silently in your mind, whisper it, or speak it aloud. It's simple yet impactful. By stating the sequence, you initiate a direct interruption to whatever disruptive thought process is running. You create a pause—a deliberate moment where you pull yourself out of the reactive mental flow and into conscious awareness.

The DivineOS sequence becomes your way of saying, "I see this thought. I choose to command it."

In that pause, you then activate the second layer of the tool: **Choice Commands**. These aren't affirmations; they are declarations of divine will, executed with the clarity and power to align your thought system with your highest self.

For example:

- If you're facing a fear of failure, you might say, "I choose to believe in my creative process."

- If you're feeling overwhelmed by responsibilities, you might command, "I choose to operate with calm clarity and trust in my timing."

- If self-doubt surfaces, remind yourself, "I choose to know my worth and my power."

These commands reinforce your intent, not as empty statements but as firm choices aligned with your divine will.

Expanding the Practice: The Role of Repetition

Engaging with this upgrade daily, especially as you listen to choice command sequences, begins to train your mind toward clarity and resilience. DivineOS offers these sequences as part of a toolkit within the Sinatia Guild, supporting your journey into a space where each experience becomes an invitation to command awareness and elevate your focus. Repetition strengthens the neural pathways that allow this self-leadership to become your standard operating mode. The process isn't merely about thinking positive; it's about building the mental habit of choosing how you think. Each time you engage with the DivineOS sequence and Choice Commands, you rewrite mental patterns, shifting from automatic reactions to deliberate responses.

Imagine the power of waking up each day, knowing you have tools to meet whatever comes your way with steady confidence. The upgrade isn't about bypassing reality; it's about choosing how you interact with it, and letting your inner command and awareness lead.

The Future Vision: Life Beyond Default Settings

What does life look like when you consistently operate in the upgraded mind matrix? You'll no longer be at the mercy of fleeting emotions or external pressures. Instead, you step into a rhythm that aligns with your internal authority, where each thought, each reaction, becomes a choice. You begin to see your life as a series of empowered moments, each one presenting an opportunity to affirm your divine potential.

In this future, you're not merely reacting to the world around you. Instead, you consciously create are consciously creating within it, crafting a life that reflects your highest values, vision, and purpose. Each day, your experience aligns more closely with what you intend, and challenges that once seemed overwhelming transform into opportunities for growth.

By moving beyond the default settings of the human operating system, you step into a divine relationship with your power—a relationship that invites you to wield that power with grace, intelligence, and purpose.

The Path of Mastery: The DivineOS Tool as a Lifelong Practice

The DivineOS sequence and Choice Commands are tools for life. As you continue to use them, you'll find that they not only help you navigate your current reality and also prepare you for new levels of growth. Just as you begin to master one level, you'll encounter new depths, new challenges, and new opportunities to deepen your understanding and embodiment of the divine.

Life will continue to bring situations that push the edges of your awareness, yet with this practice, you are not led by fear. Instead, you meet each new edge with curiosity, resilience, and a deep sense of inner authority. The DivineOS sequence helps you navigate this ever-expanding matrix of experience with the clarity of someone who understands their own system, who chooses their thoughts, and who directs their reality.

Embracing the Full Power of the Upgrade

This tool is not just a reset; it's a portal. With each use, you step through that portal into a reality that you have consciously chosen to create. You align with the 10 Dimensions of Awareness, and you reclaim your power from the hands of reaction, limitation, and doubt. In its simplicity, the DivineOS tool reveals an intricate truth: that your power is in your choice, and that choice begins in the mind.

Moving Forward: Becoming the Architect of Your Reality

As you continue forward, with 50 Choice Commands at your fingertips, you have everything you need to integrate this upgrade into your life. Use them liberally. Combine them with the DivineOS sequence as you practice daily, and watch as your internal architecture strengthens, your awareness deepens, and your reality transforms. You are no longer a passive participant in the mind matrix; you are its architect, a conscious creator stepping forward with clarity and purpose.

This is your mind upgrade. This is the beginning of your next evolution. Step forward, command your reality, and let the journey continue.

PART V
CHOICE COMMANDS

18
THE DIVINEOS SEQUENCE

Speed
Storage
Story

Senses

Security

Soul

Subconscious

Systems

Seventh sense

Sphere

19

THE 10 DIMENSIONS OF AWARENESS

Speed. Speed is my natural state. My ego is an aspect of my higher intelligence and I know how to process quickly and clearly.

Storage. I store my experiences where it best serves my system.

Story. I create the story, everything I encounter can be rewritten to serve me.

Senses. My senses are highly attuned and aware. They operate from expansion.

Security. I am safe and supported by the divine. I release fear and choose to thrive

Soul. I am always connected to what is good for my soul. My soul commands me forward into human evolution.

Subconscious. I bring to my awareness what serves ME.

Systems. I create the systems that awaken my full spectrum capacity.

Seventh Sense. My heart and Higher Intelligence are aligned. I am the seventh sense.

Sphere. I speak, learn, and live in the sphere of my own reality and creation.

20

THE POWER TO CHOOSE: THE ALCHEMY OF DECISION AND SKILL BUILDING

In a world increasingly focused on understanding the power of the mind, the hidden strength of *The New Ego Theory* and *DivineOS* isn't merely in reshaping our thought patterns—it's in equipping us with the power to choose skillfully. Beyond the metaphors and frameworks, this system offers a profound invitation to develop real human skills. Because while freedom from mental clutter and egoic traps can give us clarity, it's our choices that will truly define us.

Choosing to develop a skill—whether it's mastery of a language, a career, or even building resilience through life's challenges—creates a compounding effect. Like exercise strengthening muscles, each choice becomes a building block for confidence, generating a feedback loop of growth that doesn't rely on abstract beliefs. This loop is the proof your mind craves: as you grow, you embody your potential step by step, erasing doubts about your capacity and shifting away from self-imposed limitations.

Consider this: the journey isn't about eliminating every shadow or flaw but actively choosing to enhance our abilities, evolving from within rather than endlessly "fixing" ourselves. As *The New Ego Theory* demonstrates, simplification isn't about ignoring challenges; it's about refining our focus to free up cognitive energy for real, forward movement. Streamlining your inner narrative with deliberate, empowered choices clears the way for skill-building, confidence, and sustainable growth.

In this final chapter, the essence of *DivineOS* unfolds fully: not as a complicated system but as a simplified, powerful invitation to become intentional creators. Each choice, each command, each skill you build reinforces the notion that you are capable of navigating life from a place of empowered clarity, grounded resilience, and dynamic self-leadership. This is how we step into mastery—by consistently choosing, learning, and growing with the courage to fully embody the potential within us.

Choice as the Crucible for Alchemy

In the context of DivineOS and The New Ego Theory, alchemy is the transformation of raw, subconscious material—the beliefs, reactions, and unexamined narratives that lie beneath the surface—into refined, intentional choices. This alchemical process is about changing thoughts and reshaping the energy that fuels your actions. It's about taking subconscious matter, the patterns that typically direct our actions without conscious permission, and turning it into gold: clarity, focus, resilience, and skill.

Imagine your subconscious as a storehouse of unprocessed information, experiences, and emotions. Without direction, these materials govern us, often keeping us stuck in repetitive cycles of reaction. But through conscious choice and intention, we can extract what serves us, mold it, and discard what doesn't. We transmute the raw material of our subconscious into active, chosen qualities—like strength, skill, and purpose—that align with our highest goals.

Alchemy in this framework begins with choice. Every conscious choice you make acts like a crucible, burning away the clutter and refining your energy into a clear path forward. Each choice command you issue—statements that direct your ego's processing and instruct your mind—turns previously passive material into active force. Just as a craftsman hones raw metal into a fine instrument, you shape your potential into traits that serve you: resilience, focus, clarity, and confidence.

Through this alchemical process, you build a foundation of skills—emotional resilience, mental clarity, and creative problem-solving—essential for long-term success. Rather than chasing confidence or relying on motivation, you cultivate these qualities from within, rooted in the practiced skill of choice and focus. Each time you take subconscious matter and make a conscious choice, you reinforce a structure that grounds you in purpose and capability. Over time, this structure becomes your default way of being, setting you up for sustainable growth and success.

The power of alchemy in this context is its ability to turn every experience, thought, and feeling into fuel for your evolution. Through this transformative process, you don't just change how you see yourself—you change what you are capable of.

Mental Programming: Conscious Input for Lasting Change

The power of choice commands comes from their ability to reprogram your ego's processing patterns. This reprogramming happens through mental programming—the conscious input of specific thoughts and directives that shape how your ego interprets and responds to the world.

Here's how mental programming works in The New Ego Theory:

1 Conscious Input: You intentionally feed your ego specific thoughts, beliefs, or commands. This input acts as the programming code for your ego's processing system.

2 Repetition: The more frequently you use these commands, the stronger the neural pathways become, reinforcing the ego's processing patterns.

3 Reinforcement: As the ego processes these new inputs, it starts to align with them, creating reinforcement loops that strengthen desired behaviors or beliefs.

• Example: If you're working on developing a growth mindset, your choice command might be "I choose to learn from every challenge." By repeating this command regularly, you are programming your ego to process setbacks and difficulties as learning opportunities rather than failures. This mental programming taps into the brain's neuroplasticity —the ability of the brain to rewire itself based on new experiences and inputs

This brings us to the final, most exciting step: putting theory into action. As you've journeyed through *The New Ego Theory* and *DivineOS*, you've unlocked new ways to understand, direct, and empower yourself. Now, it's time to bridge the concepts with practice, to step into the power of intentional choices that reshape reality.

The next chapter contains a collection of 50 potent choice commands —a starting set that will help you engage and reprogram your ego for intentional growth. But this is just the beginning. *DivineOS* in its full form, offers a complete upgrade of 122 choice commands, complemented by an immersive digital experience available at Sinatia.com. This comprehensive suite includes audio meditations, workshops, and tools designed to support you in anchoring this evolution deeply into your life.

This book serves as the foundation and deep exploration of the vision behind *DivineOS*. It's a blueprint for what's possible for each person who commits to the journey and for humanity as a whole. Together, through intentional practice, we're evolving toward a world where conscious choice and empowered growth become our shared legacy.

Turn the page, step into action, and let the power to choose transform your reality.

FOUNDATIONAL SERIES

1-MEMORY

I choose to retain the data that serves me.

I choose to retain the data that serves my higher intelligence.

I choose to know what it means to allow my memory to serve me.

I choose to process data at a speed that naturally aligns with my optimum output.

I choose to feel what it means to operate at optimum output.

I choose to understand what it means to my full spectrum system to operate at optimum output.

I choose to let go of things that I am uninterested in remembering or holding onto.

I choose to release judgment about what I choose to remember.

I choose to understand what it means to live in the moment and allow my mind and operating system to serve me.

I choose to activate my memory in the most expansive definition of functionality available to me in every moment.

I choose to guide my brain to regenerate daily and achieve healthy, sharp, rich, and thriving states of operation.

I choose to know what it means to live in expression of my higher intelligence.

I choose to be activated in all aspects of cognitive connectivity.

I choose to upgrade my memory.

I choose to expand my memory.

I choose to expand how I utilize storage of data and memory.

I choose to understand what it feels like to self lead how I process data and store it in my system.

I choose to repair, rewire, and thrive in the memory of my lived reality.

I choose to repair, rewire, and thrive in the memory of my chosen reality.

I choose to repair, rewire, and thrive in the memory of my future reality.

I choose to embody a healthy, thriving memory.

I choose to understand what it means to me to decide.

I choose to understand who I am.

I choose to identify with the aspects of my memory that move me forward into my future.

I choose to evolve into the higher realms of my memory.

I choose to understand what it means to evolve into the higher realms of my memory.

I choose to remember beauty.

I choose to always remember to connect to what is good for my soul.

I choose to create from the deepest, most expansive memory of my individual truth and being.

I choose to know what it means to be who I am.

I choose to embody what it means to speak from the memory of my deepest truth.

I choose to express myself fully from all aspects of what I remember from the depth of my soul.

I choose to live as a detailed expression of my capacity.

I choose to utilize the detailed aspects of my memory.

2-Remember Choice Commands

I choose to remember who I am.

I choose to know what matters.

I choose to remember what matters to me.

I choose to remember my power.

I choose to remember my connection to my soul.

I choose to remember my innocence.

I choose to remember my pure heart.

I choose to remember how it feels to create from my pure heart.

I choose to remember the joy of creation I chose when I came here.

I choose to remember how excited I was to come here.

I choose to remember how much I love to learn here.

I choose to remember how much I love to create here.

I choose to remember how much I love myself.

I choose to remember how I support myself.

I choose to remember that I love to support myself.

I choose to remember that this is easy for me.

I choose to remember how much strength I have in my soul for creation.

I choose to remember how excited I am to create in physical reality.

I choose to remember what a gift it is to hold this form.

I choose to remember what it feels like to say YES.

I choose to remember what it feels like to say NO.

I choose to remember the power that exists inside of my YES and my NO.

I choose to remember the power that vibrates from my YES and my NO.

I choose to remember how beautiful the souls I planned to meet here are

I choose to remember that no one can make me do, feel or create anything in my life that doesn't have the capacity to serve my strength and evolution if I choose this.

I choose to remember what my free choice and will feels like in my being.

I choose to remember the divine architecture that exists in my DNA.

I choose to remember what nature is showing me about creation.

I choose to remember what I already knew about vibration, frequency, creation, energy, and my power.

I choose to remember what I already knew about sequences, templates, raw creation, and my power.

I choose to remember what I already knew about my voice, beauty, perfection, full love and acceptance in the universe.

I choose to remember why I came here to be a singular expression of the whole and I know where I stand in that relationship.

I choose to remember that I am never truly lost.

I choose to remember that I am never alone.

I choose to remember that I am always supported by the divine.

I choose to remember that there are humans and souls here that I am meant to find and create with and that I do this with the deepest joy and gratitude.

I choose to create from the memories of my deepest truth.

I choose to create from the memories of my soul.

I choose to release limited memories created from fear and trauma.

I choose to replace the space I made from the memories I released with the memories of my soul and my soul's wisdom.

I choose to create from the memories of my power.

3-Forgiveness

I choose to forgive.

I choose to release emotions that are stored in my body.

I choose to release negative stories about my past.

I choose to let go of the emotions that are connected to limited narratives from my past.

I choose to embody choice.

I choose to live in a state of potential.

I choose to understand that desperation never creates anything new.

I choose to understand that looping in victimhood never creates anything new.

I choose to understand that I chose to come here.

I choose to understand that I can receive the good in all things.

I choose to remember that I can easily return to wholeness.

I choose to feel content.

I choose to have goodwill for the souls of others.

I choose to have goodwill for the truth of others.

I choose to know the difference between my truth and the truth of others.

I choose to remember that I can say yes.

I choose to remember that I can say no.

I choose to remember that what I forgive, I release.

I choose to experience myself as complete.

I choose to understand how to set boundaries.

I choose to remember that my individual reality is separate from the external.

I choose to know my singular matrix.

I choose to experience my truth.

I choose to understand that my truth is experienced in the now.

I choose to embody a high vibrational state of perspective.

I choose to provide for myself.

I choose to transform struggle into wisdom.

I choose to create thought systems that serve me.

I choose to create thought systems that serve me in my evolution.

I choose the future moment.

I choose to remember to be aware of the now and the future moment.

I choose to remember who I am.

I choose to remember my power as a creator.

I choose to love myself.

I choose to invest in relationships that serve me.

I choose freedom.

4-Sensation

I choose to translate and experience my senses.

I choose to find potential in sensation.

I choose to connect to the genius of my sensation.

I choose to connect to my genius.

I choose to connect to my limitless potential.

I choose to enhance the language of my sensation.

I choose to find power in sensation.

I choose to understand the multidimensional capacity of my connection to sensation and create space so that I can hear it, see it, experience it, feel it, and create from it.

I choose to filter truth from story inside my relationship to sensation.

I choose to connect to the power that is inherently living, breathing, and creating in me from sensation.

I choose high vibrational sensation.

I choose to release what gets in the way of high vibrational sensation.

I choose to connect to sensation before I define reality and enhance my relationship to high level intuition.

I choose to amplify my senses in the direction of my desire.

I choose to feel high vibrational and expansive emotion in my body as my natural state.

I choose to understand how to filter and manage sensations.

I choose to direct sensations in full service to my operating system.

I choose to value, respect, and enjoy my sensations.

I choose to understand that my senses are in service to me as I am in service to them.

I choose to expand inside of my senses.

5-Power

I choose to process pure power.

I choose to regain power.

I choose to operate at optimum output.

I choose to filter programs that drain my energy and release them from my system.

I choose to release old programs with grace.

I choose to understand that connecting with my power is part of utilizing my full spectrum operating system.

I choose to replace what I release.

I choose to connect with the power of my higher intelligence.

I choose to remember that I am the higher intelligence.

I choose to understand what it means to be in communication with my higher intelligence.

I choose to operate from a state of pure intelligence.

I choose to operate from pure power.

I choose to know what it feels like to hold power.

I choose to operate from a system free of power hierarchies.

I choose to take responsibility for my power.

I choose to have faith that I am fully supported by the divine.

I choose to understand what it feels like to have access to pure states of my own power.

I choose to speak my truth.

I choose to share and speak from my heart.

I choose to understand what power means to me.

I choose to understand what my power feels like in my body.

I choose to experience my power as graceful, beautiful, and raw.

I choose to feel safe being in my power.

I choose to release old stories of powerlessness from my full spectrum system.

I choose to write stories about my life that come from my truth and power.

I choose to focus on my singular expression of power.

6-Money

I choose to know money as a dynamic field of creation.

I choose to know my position of power in relationship to money.

I choose to speak to the soul of money.

I choose to transform the role that money plays in my life as serving me in freedom.

I choose to be provided for beyond all limited internal perceptions.

I choose to release all limitation with money.

I choose to allow money to serve me.

I choose to give and allow money to flow to me and from me with ease.

I choose to have faith that I am supported by the divine.

I choose to release all fear in relationship with money.

I choose to create outside of proof.

I choose to diverge from the collective limited money narrative.

I choose to respect myself.

I choose to create from my higher intelligence in relationship to money.

I choose to expand in gratitude.

I choose to correct my perceptions of reality in line with gratitude.

I choose to have gratitude for everything that comes to me.

I choose to embody gratitude.

I choose to understand what it means to embody gratitude.

I choose to receive the good in all things.

I choose to magnetize opportunities, relationships, and experiences in my life that feel luxurious.

I choose to understand that luxury is an independent vibrational state that lives inside of me.

I choose to create cash.

I choose to create wealth.

I choose to create money.

I choose to play the game that I came here to play.

I choose to accept the game that I came here to play.

I choose to do this without heaviness.

I choose to be empowered in my relationship with money.

I choose to allow the game to be fun.

I choose to remember that this is easy.

I choose to remember that reality may feel transactional at times but my perception is not bound by this.

I choose to remember that abundance is not a zero sum game.

I choose to know that contrast creates awareness.

I choose to understand that money comes to me.

I choose to understand that money comes from me.

I choose to understand how to orient myself to a corrected source of internal power at all times.

7-Clarity

I choose to process data with clarity.

I choose to understand what it means to feel clarity in my body.

I choose to embody clarity and truth in my life.

I choose know what it feels like to be clear of illusion in my system.

I choose to know who I am.

I choose to understand the effect that knowing who I am has on my full spectrum system.

I choose to be free of the delusion of false reality constructs.

I choose to know in every moment where I stand in relationship to the reality that I am creating.

I choose to speak with clarity.

I choose to see with clarity.

I choose to understand what it feels like to hold the crisp, clear tone of clarity in my thought systems.

I choose to utilize confusion as a step towards my clarity.

I choose to understand what it looks like to see myself clearly.

I choose to see myself clearly.

I choose to understand how to lead and self guide my operating system.

I choose to guide and direct energy and awareness through my system with clarity.

I choose to feel the power of clear choice actively creating in my life.

I choose to understand what it feels like to release shrouded self perception.

I choose to feel the joy that clarity brings me.

I choose to say yes to the impact and magnetism of clear and powerful leadership.

I choose to run an operating system clear of viruses.

I choose to understand that is it my responsibility to program my system with what is good for me and my soul.

I choose to understand that I am responsible for replacing what I release in clarity.

I choose to understand that my clarity comes from knowing myself and how reality operates outside of delusion.

I choose to understand that my perception is my responsibility.

I choose to understand that my perception and vision is a power and sacred gift.

I choose to create with the universe and my life field with clarity and joy.

I choose to understand that I am safe when I see myself clearly.

I choose to bring to my vision what aligns with my accurate and clear perception.

I choose to use my full spectrum to its fullest potential.

I choose to know what it feels like to create with clarity.

I choose to create with clarity.

8-Release

I choose to release energy.

I choose to release data.

I choose to release system trauma.

I choose to release fear.

I choose to release limitation.

I choose to release shame.

I choose to release comparison.

I choose to release personas.

I choose to release disappointment.

I choose to release worry.

I choose to release anxiety.

I choose to release expectation.

I choose to keep what serves me and let go of the rest.

I choose to know what serves me.

I choose to listen to what serves me.

I choose to be in service to my evolution.

I choose to understand that it is my responsibility to replace what I release.

I choose power.

I choose peace.

I choose to embody power and peace in my system.

I choose confidence.

I choose to craft my identity.

I choose to embody all aspects of my responsibility to replace what I release.

I choose to replace what I release and fill it with what is good for my soul.

I choose to understand how to listen to what is good for my soul.

I choose to know how to identify what is good for my soul with clarity.

I choose to understand that when I release I choose to let what I release go permanently.

I choose to understand that in order to allow full release I must cultivate the good in my system.

I choose to fill myself with what is good and in alignment with my soul's truth.

I choose to be aware of the separation between myself and others from a perspective of power.

I choose to understand that I am whole.

I choose to understand that my perception is my responsibility.

I choose to understand that my perception and vision is a power and sacred gift.

I choose to create with the universe and my life field with clarity and joy.

I choose to understand that I am safe when I see myself clearly.

I choose to bring to my vision what aligns with my accurate and clear perception.

I choose to use my full spectrum to its fullest potential.

I choose to know what it feels like to create with clarity.

I choose to create with clarity.

8-Release

I choose to release energy.

I choose to release data.

I choose to release system trauma.

I choose to release fear.

I choose to release limitation.

I choose to release shame.

I choose to release comparison.

I choose to release personas.

I choose to release disappointment.

I choose to release worry.

I choose to release anxiety.

I choose to release expectation.

I choose to keep what serves me and let go of the rest.

I choose to know what serves me.

I choose to listen to what serves me.

I choose to be in service to my evolution.

I choose to understand that it is my responsibility to replace what I release.

I choose power.

I choose peace.

I choose to embody power and peace in my system.

I choose confidence.

I choose to craft my identity.

I choose to embody all aspects of my responsibility to replace what I release.

I choose to replace what I release and fill it with what is good for my soul.

I choose to understand how to listen to what is good for my soul.

I choose to know how to identify what is good for my soul with clarity.

I choose to understand that when I release I choose to let what I release go permanently.

I choose to understand that in order to allow full release I must cultivate the good in my system.

I choose to fill myself with what is good and in alignment with my soul's truth.

I choose to be aware of the separation between myself and others from a perspective of power.

I choose to understand that I am whole.

9-Connection

I choose to be connected to an internal state of divine alignment at all times.

I choose to understand what it means to be connected to my full spectrum of power.

I choose to understand what it feels like to be connected to a source of internal truth.

I choose to connect to others in love.

I choose to connect to my internal guidance.

I choose to understand what it means to be connected to my singular truth.

I choose to be connected to my genius expression.

I choose to understand what it means to connect to myself in love.

I choose to connect to myself in love.

I choose to know what it feels like to be connected in every moment.

I choose to connect to people, ideas, and accurate truths that enhance my ability to thrive.

I choose to connect with love in my life in all ways.

I choose to understand what self connection is.

I choose to understand what self connection feels like.

I choose to walk through my life field as embodied and connected to the divine.

I choose to connect with what is good for me.

I choose to connect to the good in all things.

I choose to understand what it means to connect with the good in all things.

I choose to connect to my power.

I choose to connect to the parts of me that learn fast, move through energy with ease, and create from my higher intelligence.

I choose to make connections in my mind, body, and spirit that serve my evolution.

I choose to understand what it feels like to be connected to my evolution.

I choose to be connected to my soul.

I choose to understand what it means to be connected to my soul.

I choose to connect with the ideas, systems, and awareness that create limitless possibilities in my life.

I choose to connect with the parts of me that thrive.

I choose to keep my energy clean and masterful.

I choose to connect with other souls that support me in my soul's mission.

I choose to connect to communities that allow me to be witnessed and thrive.

I choose to connect to the way that my soul thinks in harmony with my human existence and create space to hear that voice in my life.

I choose to release connections that get in the way of that.

I choose to connect and thrive.

10-Anxiety

I choose to process data and information free of anxiety.

I choose to move feelings that I interpret in my system as anxiety, quickly through my body.

I choose to understand the role that confusion plays in helping me clarify my desire.

I choose to understand how it feels in my body to be free of anxiety.

I choose to interpret sensation and information from the higher intelligence of my body in a way that serves my power and evolution.

I choose to create and relate in integrity.

I choose to understand what integrity feels like in my system.

I choose to understand that integrity is me living in my truth, not others.

I choose to keep my energy clean.

I choose to trust myself.

I choose to relate to states of power and raw energy in my system as a beautiful truth.

I choose to utilize my power.

I choose to define what joy feels like in my body.

I choose to define what freedom feels like in my body.

I choose to experience singular states of energetic responsibility.

I choose to release codependency.

I choose to replace codependency with self responsibility.

I choose to feel grounded and supported in my choice.

I choose to release confusion.

I choose to understand that confusion transforms indecision.

I choose to always receive the good from all the energy that comes into my life.

I choose to take responsibility for my energy.

I choose to remember that it is easy to take responsibility for my energy.

I choose to remember what peace feels like in my body.

I choose to allow my life to unfold in flow with my intentions.

I choose to learn how to master creation.

I choose to understand that this is my birthright.

I choose to invest in this.

I choose to remember that my life is always unfolding in a way that aligns with my intentions.

I choose to create from a place of joy.

I choose to experience the freedom in my system that allows me to create from a place of joy.

I choose to define joy in my system.

I choose to feel satisfied.

I choose to feel grateful.

I choose to understand what it feels like to embody contentment.

I choose to understand that it is easy for me to embody contentment.

I choose to understand the functional truth that contentment serves in my life.

I choose to commit to all that leads me forward into evolving from thriving.

I choose to thrive.

I choose to allow my energy to thrive.

I choose to feel calm.

I choose to understand what it feels like to embody calm and powerful energy.

I choose safety in my system.

I choose to know what it means to feel safe inside of my own power to create.

I choose to perceive my life and current situation as serving me in my pursuit to live from my higher intelligence.

I choose to make decisions.

I choose to move forward.

I choose to take action.

I choose evolution as a lifestyle.

I choose to understand that evolution as a lifestyle is my natural state.

I choose to know what it feels like to move forward in the direction of my desire while having faith.

I choose to embody faith.

I choose to remember what faith feels like in my full spectrum being.

I choose to know what it means to create from faith.

I choose to understand that I am an individual with agency.

I choose to know that I am an individual with the power of choice to be self led.

I choose to understand that I am leading my operating system forward.

I choose to create from freedom.

I choose to support myself in translating my energetic and emotional experiences in a way that serves me.

I choose to know my truth.

I choose to commit to knowing my truth.

I choose to remember that this is easy for me.

I choose to create from joy.

22

CREATION SERIES

11-Energy

I choose to process my energy with mastery.

I choose to understand what it means to master my energy.

I choose to understand what is involved in the work it requires to master my energy.

I choose to master my energy in singular states of power.

I choose to thrive.

I choose to release addictions to suffering.

I choose to replace suffering addictions with accurate perceptions of my responsibility and power.

I choose to release addictions to fear.

I choose to replace fear addictions with high vibrational energy.

I choose to understand energy in the realms of the indefinable.

I choose to define what energy creates and activates in my life field.

I choose to respect energy.

I choose to understand what it means to respect energy.

I choose to hold my relationship to energy as sacred.

I choose to understand what it means to keep my energy sacred and free.

I choose to say NO to the structures in reality that deplete my energy.

I choose to understand that what depletes my energy is in service to my awareness of what is incorrect for me.

I choose to understand what it means to be responsible for my energy.

I choose to observe energy.

I choose to be committed to an observation of energetic templates and the functional truths that are active underneath.

I choose to become aware of manipulation of energy and its purpose.

I choose to observe the purpose of energetic hierarchies.

I choose to create with my energy free of powerlessness.

I choose to connect to pure sources of energy.

I choose to create from the energy of my soul.

I choose to understand what it means to create from the energy of my soul.

I choose to develop a relationship with regenerative energy.

I choose to understand what regenerative energy means in my full spectrum system.

I choose to transform my energy into states of regenerative source.

I choose to understand what it means to me to transform my energy.

I choose to remember that this is easy for me.

I choose to allow energy to move through my system in the direction of my intentions.

I choose to commit to running clean energy through my operating system.

I choose to allow myself to release energy from my system with ease.

I choose to cultivate my energy.

I choose to replace what I release.

I choose to communicate with the energy in my life field.

I choose to value my energy.

I choose to value the energy of others.

I choose to value the individual experience I am having with my energy and my interpretation of that energy.

I choose to contribute to energy in high vibrational ways.

I choose to understand what it means to contribute to energy in high vibrational ways.

I choose to say YES and NO to energy when it is offered to me.

I choose to view my choice as the final word in my experience with energy.

I choose to create with my energy.

I choose to create from the higher realms of my energy.

I choose to understand that my energy is safe.

I choose to understand the universal truth of energy and how it moves.

I choose to understand who I am in relation to the universal truth of energy and how it moves.

I choose to create from powerful states of my own energetic perception.

I choose to remember that I am energy in motion.

I choose to remain in motion.

I choose to create from the future moment.

12-Psychic abilities

I choose to see with my senses.

I choose to see through my senses.

I choose to see in tune with my senses.

I choose to see in harmony with my senses.

I choose to see reality through my full spectrum system.

I choose to see through reality with my full spectrum system.

I choose to process reality through a corrected lens.

I choose to sense, see, feel, and understand the higher level conversation about me that is coming from me.

I choose to enhance my perception.

I choose to upgrade my psychic abilities.

I choose to upgrade my psychic abilities in a way that aligns with my soul blueprint.

I choose to see what is for me.

I choose to see only what is for me.

I choose to become aware of where I look.

I choose to understand the importance of discernment.

I choose to keep my energy clean.

I choose to run my operating system free of distortion.

I choose to stay grounded.

I choose to understand what it means to stay grounded.

I choose to understand what it feels like in my body to stay grounded.

I choose to understand the purpose of all things that happen in my life.

I choose to create from my seventh sense.

I choose to know that I am the seventh sense.

I choose to know that I am the timeline.

I choose to connect to the timeline that I am experiencing, projecting, and connected to at all times.

I choose to know that I can sense when I am aligned with time.

I choose to know how to master time.

I choose to master creation.

I choose to master manifestation.

I choose to see clearly.

I choose to release codependency.

I choose to understand how to create and ask myself the right questions.

I choose to know how to connect to what matters to me.

I choose to know what matters to me.

I choose to create from what matters to me.

I choose to see what matters to me.

13-Manifestation

I choose to define manifestation.

I choose to define manifestation as creation.

I choose to understand that how I create is a manifestation of the dimensions in me that are active, inactive, conscious, subconscious, and perceptive.

I choose to understand that manifestation is my birthright.

I choose to understand that I am creating here, with my soul.

I choose to understand that I am creating here, with my human.

I choose to understand that manifestation is an individual field of creation.

I choose to know that I create in my own unique way.

I choose to know that I am a unique creation of the divine.

I choose to understand that I am a divine love affair.

I choose to write new stories.

I choose to create from my dreams.

I choose to create from the parts of me that are soul led.

I choose to create from the parts of me that are high vibrational.

I choose to release fear about what I create.

I choose to understand how intention functions in my life.

I choose to know that mastering this, is the journey.

I choose to take responsibility for what I create.

I choose to take ownership of my life and what I create in my life.

I choose to perceive my life as correct in every moment so that I can develop wisdom.

I choose to become aware of wisdom as an active, walking, force of creation in my life.

I choose to understand that concepts that I embody turn into walking knowledge.

I choose to understand that knowledge is not wisdom.

I choose to accept that thinking about what I desire and never taking action, is a deluded and ignorant way to live.

I choose to understand that never taking action is ignorant because my system is intelligent.

I choose to respect myself.

I choose to know that I can transform.

I choose to do this free of suffering.

I choose to use challenges as opportunities.

I choose to understand the purpose of chaos in my life.

I choose to accept that I never learn lessons from fear.

I choose to release shame connected to functional truth.

I choose to see the difference between the stories I tell myself about failure is completely different than the mechanisms active in creation.

I choose to know that accepting functional truth is never a judgment of personal value.

I choose to take responsibility for how I perceive myself.

I choose to take responsibility for how I perceive the world.

I choose to accept that if I agree to a narrative about my personal failure, I am the one who is responsible for changing this.

I choose to understand the power of perception.

I choose to accept the power of perspective.

I choose to take responsibility for how I look at things.

I choose to look at things that interest me.

I choose to invest in learning how to manifest in alignment with my true nature.

I choose to appreciate this gift.

I choose to never take this gift for granted.

I choose to always remember to look at the tiny moments with potential.

I choose to understand the power of gratitude.

I choose to understand gratitude as a high vibrational field for transformation.

I choose to connect with the wisdom available to me that comes from me so that I can master creation.

I choose to create.

14-Freedom

I choose to honor myself.

I choose to see myself as open and free.

I choose to ask myself what freedom means to me.

I choose to define my understanding of freedom as a learnable, livable, long lasting practice of expansion and embodiment.

I choose to know that I am safe here.

I choose to honor my inner rhythm.

I choose to know what inner rhythm feels like in my body.

I choose to know that I am free.

I choose to know that I am free to choose.

I choose to understand that my freedom is independent of the freedom of others.

I choose to feel myself soar.

I choose to connect to a sensation in my body that feels limitless.

I choose to understand how I limit myself.

I choose to accept that the stories I tell myself about who I am and what I am capable of can create cages around me.

I choose to know that I am the only one who can set myself free.

I choose to allow my spirit to express freely.

I choose to release all forms of self judgment about how I have reacted to freedom in my past, present, and future.

I choose to ask myself who has control over me.

I choose to ask myself if the limited answers I receive are true.

I choose to accept the truth that my essence is made of freedom.

I choose to understand how to connect to the essence of my truth.

I choose to consider that the rules I choose to accept in all moments of my life can change when I allow them to.

I choose to make my own rules.

I choose to respect the laws of energy.

I choose to explore the edges of limitation in me as opportunities to expand into more freedom.

I choose to observe my relationship to freedom.

I choose to hold this energy with grace.

I choose to respect freedom.

I choose to value my freedom more than I value my stories of oppression.

I choose to understand that when I make this choice, I am not condoning distorted power hierarchies.

I choose to know that I can always create new stories.

I choose to understand that my definition of I am, is my prophecy.

I choose to release victimhood from my conscious awareness.

I choose to see, sense, feel, and experience the difference between the stories I tell myself about who I am and who I am meant to be.

I choose to be curious.

I choose to take responsibility for creating my life.

I choose to remove and release the way I speak about myself in all moments to align with the inherent freedom I have to create in my life.

I choose to release complaining.

I choose to release any addiction I have to complaining as a source of self support.

I choose to give myself a break.

I choose to give myself a break before I feel the need to complain about what is happening, not happening, available, not available, or impressed unwillingly upon me as circumstances of my reality.

I choose to see how what I intend, I receive.

I choose to understand that I define how I receive what comes to me.

I choose to see the freedom in that.

I choose to observe how I can actionably live in a state of freedom.

I choose to commit to talking about my life, how I experience my life, and how I take action in my life from a perspective of freedom.

I choose to set myself free.

15-Shapes

I choose to think in shapes.

I choose to know what it feels like to think in shapes.

I choose to see patterns of creation active in my life, speaking to me about what I am creating in the world.

I choose to see the perfect and divine structures in shapes.

I choose to observe the sphere.

I choose to consider its shape.

I choose to listen to what it has to say to me, about me, about nature, about creation, about the nature of my creation.

I choose to see the perfection in that.

I choose to observe the cube.

I choose to consider its shape.

I choose to listen to what it has to say to me, about me, about nature, about creation, about the nature of my creation.

I choose to see the perfection in that.

I choose to observe the triangle.

I choose to consider its shape.

I choose to listen to what it has to say to me, about me, about nature, about creation, about the nature of my creation.

I choose to see the perfection in that.

I choose to observe the horizon.

I choose to consider its shape.

I choose to listen to what it has to say to me, about me, about nature, about creation, about the nature of my creation.

I choose to see the perfection in that.

I choose to observe my reality.

I choose to consider its shape.

I choose to listen to what it has to say to me, about me, about nature, about creation, about the nature of my creation.

I choose to see the perfection in that.

I choose to see the shape of my words.

I choose to observe how they move.

I choose to consider the language of shapes, as in motion.

I choose to know that how I speak and what I speak creates shapes around me.

I choose to see the perfection in that.

I choose to see emotion in shapes.

I choose to accept that my emotions create shapes around me.

I choose to see my sacred geometric self.

I choose to take responsibility for the shapes that I hold in my field.

I choose to see how my shape responds, interacts with, and creates with the other shapes in reality.

I choose to see the perfection in that.

I choose to see myself as separate.

I choose to see myself as whole.

I choose to consider the angles.

I choose to know what it feels like in my body to consider the angles.

I choose to upgrade my consciousness to speak and feel love into creation as a mathematical language of connection that creates equations of my lived and energetic experience.

I choose to consider what is possible in that.

I choose to understand what it feels like in my body to speak the language of nature.

I choose to consider the shapes.

I choose to interact with the elements, both earth bound and cosmic as I engage with my higher intelligence.

I choose to think multidimensionally.

I choose to observe multidimensionally.

I choose to allow myself to learn new languages.

I choose to consider what is possible for me when I speak to creation from all levels of my divine capacity.

16-Jealousy

I choose to release jealousy.

I choose to understand that I am already connected to everything that I desire.

I choose to know the purpose of my desire.

I choose to accept that desire is what ignites my energetic template for creation.

I choose to know what it feels like in my body to have what I desire.

I choose to anticipate receiving what I desire as a complete and full return to my natural state as a creator.

I choose to shift sensations of inadequacies into states of internal knowing.

I choose to understand that indications of jealousy are invitations to creation.

I choose to know that I am the one who says yes and no.

I choose to look at perspectives in my life that create deficits from all angles.

I choose to know what those angles feel like in my body.

I choose to become aware of the vast and limitless resources of potential that are orbiting my field.

I choose to live free of removal.

I choose to accept a life free of removal.

I choose to say yes to a life that I craft, cultivate, and create.

I choose to support myself.

I choose to provide me with what I need to feel whole.

I choose to support myself emotionally within a template of love that provides me with the connection I seek and desire.

I choose to understand that I am not alone.

I choose to connect to the fabric of my singular matrix.

I choose to see myself as whole, as part of the whole, as separate and supported.

I choose to release need.

I choose to live free of need.

I choose to understand that need can become desire.

I choose to look at my life as a rich and perfect relationship full of provision.

I choose to see the next opportunity.

I choose to celebrate the success of others.

I choose to do this because I understand that in doing so, I connect to a transformative field of vibration that increases my capacity to have, hold, and create.

I choose this because it is natural for me to do so.

I choose to release distortion.

I choose to operate from clean emotion.

I choose to understand what it feels like in my body to celebrate what I have.

I choose to see what I have as a unique gift.

I choose to see myself as an individual universe of beauty.

I choose to perceive, connect to, and live from that beauty.

I choose to have what I can hold.

I choose to hold my dreams.

I choose my dreams.

17-The home

I choose to remember the home.

I choose to know that I am home.

I choose to know the home that lives in the body.

I choose to know that my body is the current home of my soul.

I choose to feel safe here.

I choose to remember that I chose to come here.

I choose to know what it feels like to be home.

I choose to connect to a feeling of relaxed, open, supported, and excited energy in my body that fuels my internal source of joy.

I choose to connect with a sensation of peace.

I choose to know what peace feels like in my body.

I choose to allow this place in me to feel like a deep and endless blossoming sigh of purpose and pleasure.

I choose to cultivate a deep and visceral connection with my nervous system.

I choose to align with a soul oriented nervous system that naturally regulates itself in perfect and optimal use of my full spectrum system.

I choose to release pain, desperation, disappointment, shame, and judgment from my body.

I choose to hold myself.

I choose to remember the home.

I choose to remember the home that I came from.

I choose to remember the dimension of me that is connected to the fabric of love weaving all of life together as the miracle.

I choose to know that I am a miracle.

I choose to feel this essence in my body.

I choose to breathe life from this essence and allow it to remind me in every moment of who I truly am.

I choose this remembrance in clarity.

I choose to embrace this free of confusion.

I choose to know what it feels like in my body to hold this identity.

I choose to accept that I am from here, free of here, connected here, and connected elsewhere beyond time and limitation and I choose this as a movement of truth in my life.

I choose to accept that I am more than one thing.

I choose to accept that I am many things.

I choose to accept that I am one thing.

I choose to feel in my body that all the things that I am, perhaps undefinable at times, are defined by me through my awareness.

I choose to see the perfection in that.

I choose to understand that I can hold time in my body and experience it as a keeper of my own singular wisdom.

I choose to remember the home.

I choose to remember the stardust.

I choose to remember the sand.

I choose to remember the cosmos.

I choose to stand on this earth.

I choose to touch the waters of my consciousness.

I choose to allow the physical elements available to me here, where I am now, where I choose to be, as a comfort and connection to matter.

I choose to know that I matter.

I choose to create with matter.

I choose to understand what it feels like in my body to be both matter and essence.

I choose to celebrate the potential in that.

I choose to remember the home.

I choose be the home.

I choose to be home.

I choose the home.

18-Patterns

I choose to focus on the patterns.

I choose to comprehend the patterns active in me that are creating my reality.

I choose to comprehend the patterns active in the universe that are assisting me in creating my reality.

I choose to comprehend the patterns active in the collective that are operating in contrast to my reality.

I choose to see how these patterns are unique, separate, connected, and defined.

I choose to connect to the sequence.

I choose to observe the behavior of energy as it moves through patterns, with patterns, and in response to patterns.

I choose to understand the fabric of patterns.

I choose to touch my fingers to the weaving.

I choose to know what it feels like in my body to move with the fibers of creation.

I choose to learn how to dance in its rhythm.

I choose to move freely.

I choose to cultivate an identity that operates within the explorative field of creation as an architect of patterns that align with my higher intelligence.

I choose to see the threads.

I choose to see the connections.

I choose to feel the connections in my body.

I choose to interpret the divine wisdom of connections in my body.

I choose to upgrade the patterns in my DNA.

I choose to know what it feels like in my body to accelerate.

I choose to become the command.

I choose to know, free from the invitation of what is comfortable, old, worn out, and false, the truth of solutions as possibility releases me from the past.

I choose to create from that freedom.

I choose to pay attention to patterns as moldable, ever evolving, and true connected to how I live my life and how I interact with universal law.

I choose to upgrade my internal patterning.

I choose to focus on my habits.

I choose to create from crystal clear awareness connected to the patterns I am choosing in my life and the patterns I require in order to elevate my vibration.

I choose to understand that there are patterns active in my life field that are ready to release.

I choose to know what it feels like to release old patterns in my body.

I choose to release old patterns in my body.

I choose to focus on what I create.

I choose to create from high vibrational patterns of creation.

I choose to know that patterns in my past are not predictions of my future.

I choose to know that I am the prophecy.

I choose to play within the realm of pattern creation as a game.

I choose to remember what it feels like to play.

I choose to activate my higher intelligence to observe patterns, use them to create, and stay focused and aware of my heart's desire.

I choose to become the pattern.

19-Alignment

I choose to say yes to alignment.

I choose to align to my truth.

I choose to align to my soul mission work.

I choose to align to the people in my life who are meant for me.

I choose to align to the magic that I am here to create in the world.

I choose to understand alignment as the adjustments of my choices, awareness, and energies.

I choose to let alignment be simple.

I choose to release frustration about how I align to what I desire to create in my life.

I choose to understand that alignment comes from alchemy.

I choose to understand that alignment comes from my choices.

I choose to understand that alignment comes from my energy.

I choose to understand that alignment comes from how I see myself and how I connect my Identity to the way that I am being, living, and expressing in my life.

I choose alignment.

I choose to know that when I align to my synchronistic field, the conversations that life is attempting to have with me about what I desire to create becomes crystal clear.

I choose alignment in the tiny moments.

I choose to know how to make the tiny adjustments that activate massive shifts in my desired reality.

I choose to understand that all awarenesses connected to alignment are within my reach.

I choose to take responsibility for aligning to the things that I desire to create and accept that if I refuse to do so, I will experience exactly what is there for me now.

I choose to understand that my perception can change in an instant.

I choose to accept that my perspective creates my perception.

I choose to perceive alignment in my life field.

I choose to say yes to what is aligned for me, in all moments and free myself from ignoring what is ready to be released in my field.

I choose to let go.

I choose to know what it feels like to let go in my body.

I choose to know what it feels like to let go.

I choose courage.

I choose to have the courage to say no to what is not aligned with the higher soul frequencies available to me, that are from me, and part of my soul blueprint.

I choose to live free of dismissal.

I choose to fine tune my awareness.

I choose to know what it feels like in my body to hold a high level awareness of energy, intention, and action and I choose this because it is natural for me to do so.

I choose to see the orbits active in my field, sparked my by intention, fueled by my soul capacity, and aligned in my human vibration.

I choose to do the work.

I choose to do the work and live free of feeling burdened by opportunity.

I choose to accept that if I say I desire to create big things in the world, I live free of being a victim of my own creation.

I choose to accept that my life field believes me.

I choose to accept that my magic believes me.

I choose to accept that my Identity believes me.

I choose to understand that when I speak about myself in a way that does not align with my soul frequency, my human capacity crafts a narrative in my field that takes living shape in my life.

I choose to understand that my choices are connected to my alignment

I choose to understand that my action is connected to my alignment.

I choose to know what the dynamic, evolving, and every growing field of alignment feels like in my lived experience and I choose to live courageously.

I choose to know that when I make decisions, big or small, based on the alignment available to me in my soul's frequency, I will be supported in the transition from where I am now to where I am going.

I choose to take advantage of this opportunity.

I choose to live free of fear.

I choose to understand what alignment means as an embodied active, moment to moment series of choices and awarenesses in my life.

I choose to move.

20-Creation

I choose to create.

I choose to know myself as creation.

I choose to follow a logical and applicable thought process that leads me to the awareness that if I am in fact creation, then my most natural gift is that of a creator.

I choose to accept those gifts.

I choose to create my reality.

I choose to know the difference between the now moment and the future moment.

I choose to become aware that the intentions I apply to my future moment create the frame for how I am experiencing the now moment.

I choose to release distortion connected to apathetic energy in my field for creation.

I choose to release blame.

I choose to release powerlessness.

I choose to accept that what I release, I must replace with what is good for my soul.

I choose to know that it is good for my soul to create here.

I choose to understand that this is why I came here.

I choose to know what it feels like in my body to create from my soul capacity.

I choose to know myself.

I choose to observe how I create emotion in my body.

I choose to observe how emotions are translated by my mind.

I choose to observe the narrative I am crafting that tells me what I am capable and incapable of creating.

I choose to integrate.

I choose to ask myself if how I am engaging in creation is serving me in my fullest capacity.

I choose to accept the answer I receive and do something about it.

I choose to take action.

I choose to build my capacity to hold the energy that is required to receive what I desire to create.

I choose to define manifestation as creation.

I choose to create with conscious awareness.

I choose to invest in my growth as an individual in mind, body, and spirit to expand my capacity for creation and assist my human in growing into a high vibrational state that I can hold.

I choose to ask myself, if I instantly had access to everything that I desire to create free of effort, challenge, or personal growth, what would my purpose be on this Earth?

I choose to sit quietly in that truth.

I choose to make my life sacred.

I choose to master intentional living.

I choose to correct my processing to align with my higher intelligence.

I choose to correct my energy connected to wealth, money, and thriving.

I choose to invest in mastering my magic.

I choose technical magic.

I choose to understand that a life free of growth and challenge is a life free of personal evolution.

I choose to know I came here to evolve.

I choose to learn what I need to know to master my natural ability to manifest, that is of me, created by me, and ignited by my highest soul frequency.

I choose to do what it takes to raise my vibration so that my human can turn challenge into personal power.

I choose to understand that this is my journey.

I choose to experience this journey with gratitude and the gift of giving me what I ask for.

I choose to create here.

FREEDOM SERIES

21-Faith

I choose to know faith.

I choose to open my energetic template to the template of divine faith and provision.

I choose to know that when I activate an intention in my life that is aligned with my soul mission I am supported by my faith.

I choose to know that faith is an aspect of the divine.

I choose to develop a relationship with faith that carries me forward in connection to my magic.

I choose to see the difference between faith and hope.

I choose to know faith as the divine horizon.

I choose to step into new foundations.

I choose to step into a new path.

I choose to release distorted patterns of faith active in the collective and free myself from delusion.

I choose to know what faith feels like in my body.

I choose to cultivate faith in every step, every action, every belief, and every dream I have for how much incredible magic I can create here on Earth.

I choose to accept that faith is a gateway.

I choose to know faith as a wisdom keeper.

I choose to use faith as a key to unlock deeper awareness of my capacity.

I choose to feel the energy of faith filling my body, mind, and spirit with fuel for creation.

I choose to know where to put my faith.

I choose to put my faith in myself and in the divine.

I choose to know that faith in myself and in the divine activates my movement into the unknown aspects of what I already own, am creating, and moving in motion with.

I choose to have faith.

I choose to know that I am in the right place at the right time, equipped with the agency to take action in the direction that is correct for me.

I choose to move forward moment to moment in the cultivation of my internal strength that proves to me through my motion that I am worthy of faith in myself.

I choose to cultivate this motion as energy and fuel for my creation.

I choose to feel peace.

I choose to feel peace in the unknown.

I choose to feel peace in the unknown because I have faith in myself and in the divine.

I choose to observe faith as a tool of recollection.

I choose to recall my power as a creator.

I choose to know that when I engage in creating the reality I desire, I am the one who proves to my system that I can do what I dream.

I choose to create without proof.

I choose to know that I am the proof.

I choose to move forward knowing that I am capable of unimaginable magic.

I choose to know that my magic comes from within.

I choose to know that from within, I have access to a deep well of wisdom, self provision, and embodied magic that I can discover through the motion of creation.

I choose to see the motion of creation active in my life.

I choose to discover what skills I can develop in this process.

I choose to know that the development of human resilience connected to how I create is the journey I have set myself upon when I say yes to the path of soul led self discovery.

I choose to lead myself forward with faith.

22-Emotions

I choose to understand the purpose of emotion as a creator.

I choose to feel the flow of emotion in my body.

I choose to know what emotion feels like in my body for creation.

I choose to observe emotion from a different lens.

I choose to cultivate high value emotion.

I choose to understand that manifestation happens in the body.

I choose to know that my body believes the way that it feels when it is experiencing emotion.

I choose to know that this experience is free of mental translation, logic, and my higher intelligence if I do not apply this awareness to the processing of emotion in my system.

I choose to understand that emotion tells a story in my body.

I choose to move emotion through my being in an intentional manner.

I choose to ask myself, where is the origin of emotion in me?

I choose to ask myself if my emotions are true.

I choose to contemplate the distance between my ability to craft a narrative in my life that is free, empowered, sovereign….and the emotions that I create as a result of that narrative.

I choose to observe emotion.

I choose to ask myself, if I am experiencing painful, limiting, dramatic, and disempowered emotions, do I allow them to define my experience.

I choose to be honest with myself about my Souls capacity.

I choose to know the emotions of my soul.

I choose to live from this place.

I choose to cultivate high value emotion.

I choose to seed emotion in my life through a practice of grace, gratitude, recognition of safety, provision, internal peace, and wholeness that blossoms into regenerative energy I create with.

I choose to flow.

I choose to understand that reality flows in the direction of my awareness.

I choose to understand that my reality believes me.

I choose to understand that my body believes me.

I choose to create cohesion in my system between my mind, heart, and spirit that unearths the good in my life.

I choose to experience the emotions of my soul.

I choose to ask myself if soul emotions behave differently than human centered emotions.

I choose to know what that feels like in my body.

I choose to use emotion as fuel for creation.

I choose to know that I am a creator.

I choose to understand that if I choose to engage in alchemy from low vibrational emotions that I am transforming the substance of that essence into a distilled and concentrated form created from the emotion I engage with.

I choose to contemplate what is a more powerful and useful investment within that context.

I choose to take cues from the emotion in my body and spirit as an indicator that I am a magician, on the path to higher frequencies and sustained states of creation because it is my desire to do so.

I choose to accept what I feel and give myself grace.

I choose to create what I desire to feel and give myself grace.

I choose to know that this is my choice.

I choose to know that I am supported by the divine.

I choose to release emotion.

I choose to release shame.

I choose to release judgment.

I choose to evolve.

I choose to evolve with the freedom of self awareness and sovereign cultivated states of feeling that propel me forward in the direction of my desire.

I choose to experience bliss.

I choose to feel all of the soul magic that I am here to embody.

I choose to value this gift.

I choose to upgrade my emotions.

I choose to live in the miraculous fibers of love.

23-Courage

I choose to have courage.

I choose to develop courage in my system that aligns with the desire I hold to live authentically.

I choose to know that I am accepted.

I choose to know what it feels like in my body to accept myself.

I choose to question how much is truly at risk.

I choose to look at the fear that lives in me connected to personas of the self that I am enslaved to.

I choose to ask myself if I desire to continue living in this manner.

I choose to take to heart the answer that I receive and do something about it.

I choose to express myself fully.

I choose to feel the rawness of me.

I choose to live from my raw and unfiltered self with grace.

I choose to cultivate high value emotion.

I choose to cultivate high value connections.

I choose to cultivate my truth.

I choose to see the separation between myself, my judgment of self, and the blame I put on others for how much I am willing to share.

I choose to look at the correctness of my life field in that regard and have courage to see what needs to be seen.

I choose to release offense.

I choose to understand that observations of perceived offense, outrage, shame, and judgment are opportunities to correct my internal system to develop courage for creation.

I choose to correct my perception to view all opportunities for transformation in releasing personas as a step towards my true identity.

I choose to know that I am the one responsible for crafting my identity.

I choose to see this as a gift.

I choose to know that when I speak from my true and authentic self, that I have the opportunity to connect to people who are aligned with the dimension of reality that I am designed with purpose to exist from.

I choose to experience this opportunity for connection as a constellation of singular universes in orbit creating together with the intentions of our souls to co-create here.

I choose to see my responsibility in that.

I choose to take responsibility for having courage.

I choose to know that I am always supported by the divine.

I choose to know that when I say yes to a path of soul expansion and creation, my job as a human is to continue to build skill and develop internal states of resilience.

I choose to see this as an opportunity to stand up for what I believe in.

I choose to believe in myself.

I choose to believe in my magic.

I choose to know that when I believe in myself, myself believes me back.

I choose to know that when I believe in my magic, my magic believes me back.

I choose to recognize the intricate, functional, and pragmatic application of these statements.

I choose to know what it feels like in my body to be essenced in my self belief.

I choose to observe the truth that in moments when I am experiencing doubt, courage carries me forward.

I choose to have courage in my creation.

24-Apathy

I choose to release apathy.

I choose to understand the energetic template of apathy and how it impacts humanity, creation, and magic as I define it in my life.

I choose to observe.

I choose to understand that apathy is the lowest vibrational form of energy on earth.

I choose to ask myself why this is true.

I choose to consider apathy in connection to reactions.

I choose to consider apathy in connection to desire.

I choose to consider apathy in connection to creation.

I choose to consider apathy in connection to motion.

I choose to consider apathy in connection to evolution.

I choose to ask myself what compels me forward.

I choose to find my passion.

I choose to find my purpose.

I choose to connect to the open and ever expanding fractal of my existence as a raw and revolutionary catalyst of creation.

I choose to ask myself what I am here to inspire.

I choose to ask myself what inspires me into the motion of magic and purpose that sets me on a path of creation and fuels me in every moment.

I choose to become this.

I choose to become this and more.

I choose to take responsibility for the dreams that I hold in my heart.

I choose to welcome the fluctuations of energy and experience that I hold in my being as a weaver of reality.

I choose to see the perfection in that.

I choose to ask myself what it means in my body to detach.

I choose to observe the functional truth of detachment from an empowered perspective and feel the nuance of choice versus deflection.

I choose to understand that I can hold what I create.

I choose to know what it feels like in my body to hold what I create.

I choose to commit to the stream of soul potential that flows through me.

I choose to observe that when I initiate myself on a path of creation from my soul frequency that challenge arises to provide me with the energy I require to create.

I choose to define challenge as opportunity.

I choose to release overwhelm from my life field.

I choose to understand that indecision is a decision.

I choose to know what it feels like in my body to decide.

I choose to ask myself, if it is truly a matter of making the right decision in my life or if, it is rather about making the decision right in myself.

I choose to pay attention to the difference.

I choose to know the difference between aligning myself to what I desire over waiting for alignment to find me.

I choose to release seeking.

I choose to be the finder of me.

I choose to ask myself the right questions and apply definitions of functional truth before I allow my system to adopt identities that are false, delusional and confused.

I choose to consider how confusion affects my decisions.

I choose to consider how confusion affects sensations of self guidance.

I choose to consider how confusion operates as alchemy in my life.

I choose to ask myself how intentional I am about using elevated states of consciousness and creation that put me on the path of personal evolution that I claim to walk upon.

I choose to claim my magic.

I choose devotion to my heart.

I choose to live from my desire.

I choose to thrive.

I choose life.

25-Functional Truth

I choose to develop a deep internal relationship to truth.

I choose to know what that feels like in my body.

I choose to consider the concept of functional truth.

I choose to observe that there is human truth, divine truth, and mechanical truth.

I choose to pay attention to how truth operates in the collective.

I choose to pay attention to how truth operates in me.

I choose to experience a singular definition of truth that moves in reality as a sequence of behavior showing me the operation of all things great and small.

I choose to know how this perspective serves me.

I choose to understand truth in shapes.

I choose to know the functional truth of the sphere.

I choose to know the functional truth of time.

I choose to know the functional truth of the paradox.

I choose to know the functional truth of vibration.

I choose to know the functional truth of frequency.

I choose to see the difference between the truth that resonates with me on one degree of my experience and the truth that resonates with me in the ancient aspects of my Soul lineage.

I choose to question how it operates.

I choose to know my truth and allow myself to oscillate between the multidimensional nature of truth, my choice to engage in truth, and the truth that is being presented to me as truth.

I choose to contemplate ultimate truth.

I choose to allow that truth to take me on journeys into the distant and right here moments while navigating the space between as a means to unlock higher aspects of my divine experience here on Earth.

I choose to respect the truth of others and let them have it.

I choose to speak up about what is true for me.

I choose to do this with awareness and high levels of integrity that continue to allow me to grow into what I am, what I am meant to become, and what I was in all timelines of conscious expression.

I choose to feel truth when words are spoken to me.

I choose to feel truth in what I encounter.

I choose to experience this sensation in proximity to what exists outside of me and inside of me.

I choose to know its matter.

I choose to understand that claiming to know, integrating what I know, and living what I know are not the same thing.

I choose to ask better questions.

I choose to learn to think in new ways that enhance my relationship to creation.

I choose to step into flow with my Identity and my soul self as a functional mechanism of what it takes to be a creator.

I choose to know myself as a creator.

I choose to allow this to be my deepest truth.

I choose to create what is good, true, and powerful in this world.

I choose to understand the space between layers of truth, behaviors of truth, and energies of truth as alchemy.

I choose to transform.

I choose to rise in my truth.

26-Identity

I choose to craft my Identity.

I choose to separate my programming from my Identity.

I choose to allow myself to be fluid in my relationship to my Identity in a state of ever evolving truth and empowerment.

I choose to ask myself why my full spectrum system depends on identifying definitions of identity and what it serves in me.

I choose to ask myself how my full spectrum system depends on identifying definitions of identity and what it serves in me.

I choose to ask myself if I am using this mechanism to my advantage.

I choose to know that my Identity is not dependent on how others perceive me.

I choose to acknowledge that no one can give me permission to fully see myself.

I choose to acknowledge that no one can give me permission to fully express myself.

I choose to acknowledge that no one can give me permission to fully embody myself.

I choose to know that only I can love myself.

I choose to know that only I can free myself.

I choose to know that only I can know myself.

I choose to know how the symptoms of distorted self Identity operate in my body.

I choose to ask myself if the reflections I see in the eyes of others could ever truly define my perspective of the self.

I choose to commit to myself.

I choose to commit to seeing what I am capable of.

I choose to admit to myself what I truly desire when connecting to others.

I choose to see the beauty of connection.

I choose to accept that I can always receive the good in connection and release what does not align with my definitions of self, free of loss.

I choose to release persona.

I choose to ask myself to experience in a clean, clear, and empowered energetic template the difference between persona, personality, and Identity.

I choose to experience my Soul Identity.

I choose to know that living free of fear is a gift to myself and those who connect with me.

I choose to challenge the mainstream narrative of the ego.

I choose to consider that every bit of information my system is attempting to relate back to me has value.

I choose to ask myself what I value.

I choose to create an Identity based on what I value, what I choose to focus on, what serves me, and what feels true in my system.

I choose to expand.

I choose expansion into the limitless potential of my soul frequency as the motion of my Identity.

I choose to release what gets in the way of that.

I choose to be my full self.

I choose to operate from a full spectrum system integrating and expressing everything that I am with clarity, potency, and deep self knowledge.

I choose to say yes to myself.

I choose to say no to what is no longer.

I choose to release this with grace and fluid motion.

I choose to release across all timelines, the present, and the future of me, in all moments, in before moments, in this moment, all times, every time.

I choose to know who I am, who I choose to be, and who I have always been.

27-Divine Principles

I choose to rest my life upon the divine horizon.

I choose to find peace and faith in knowing that I am supported.

I choose to understand that when I say yes to my soul promise, my life begins moving in motion with divine law and I am held to the borders and boundaries of my human capacity.

I choose to have faith.

I choose to have faith and move forward.

I choose to understand that every time I take a step forward in faith, I am strengthening the core of my internal architecture.

I choose to know nature.

I choose to know nature and its elements.

I choose to live with nature, with my nature, and the force that binds us in love as a still and comprehensive ecosystem of awareness.

I choose love for this Earth.

I choose gratitude for everything that I have here and now.

I choose to be present with myself.

I choose courage.

I choose love.

I choose to express myself.

I choose to understand what it feels like in my body to engage with divine truth.

I choose to know divine principles as active supportive structures and geometries that are alive and active in my life field.

I choose to see beyond narratives.

I choose to accept the promise that lives inside of my soul to align with the life that god, nature, this earth, my human body, and the divine has intended for me.

I choose to take this up as my quest.

I choose to enjoy sensation.

I choose to enjoy the sensation of higher frequencies moving through me and pushing me towards growth to live, create, and express from the higher realms.

I choose to actualize my promise.

I choose to understand that when I make a promise to myself, I should intentionally order my life to keep that promise so that I can make full use of the magic that is here to provide for me.

I choose to see myself as whole and complete.

I choose to make these awarenesses come to life in tiny moments of self doubt, lack, lostness, and aloneness in order to return to my rightful place as the creator of my reality.

I choose to ask myself what it looks like when I am thriving and living from a place of pure love and magic in my life.

I choose to walk supported.

I choose to invest in building the internal structures that house the holy other that is part of my divine nature.

I choose to understand the raw, real, sharp, gracious, and chaotic nature of the divine and make peace with the natural order of the universe so that I don't live in opposition to it.

I choose to move with the will of the divine.

I choose to create in shapes.

I choose to learn how to choose what has chosen me.

I choose to understand that non linear and linear structures evolve and devolve in my system depending on how I use the mechanisms of reality that are in operation around me.

I choose to know that I am the only one who can build up the laws inside of myself that guide me on how to utilize these mechanisms.

I choose worship.

I choose exaltation.

I choose high vibration.

I choose my soul frequency.

I choose ritual.

I choose to hold sacred.

I choose to stand up.

I choose to look myself eye to eye.

I choose to find my power.

I choose to become all that I am, all that I was, and all that I will be.

I choose to know my name.

28-The Cube

I choose to know the divine and holy architecture of the cube.

I choose to see all sides.

I choose to know my side.

I choose to engage in the physical aspects of life with joy, emotion, groundedness, and empowerment.

I choose to see this as a gift.

I choose to create spaces in my life where I can experience equality free of force, lack, and comparison.

I choose to stand equal to my own gifts.

I choose to stand equal to my own potential.

I choose to stand equal to my own sovereign will.

I choose to become deeply rooted in the freedom of seeing what I am equal to and the understanding that there is no reduction in proximity unless I am the one who has chosen to diminish myself.

I choose to work with the elements.

I choose to know the power of one.

I choose to know the power of two.

I choose to know the power of three.

I choose to know the power of four.

I choose to know the power of seven.

I choose to become the center point.

I choose to understand myself as multidimensional.

I choose to process data with clean, clear, and correct thinking systems that allow me to emerge as expansive consciousness in relation to the whole.

I choose to take responsibility for my space.

I choose to take responsibility for my energy.

I choose to take responsibility for my words.

I choose to take responsibility for what I create in the world.

I choose to take responsibility for my freedom.

I choose to take responsibility for my gracious treatment of myself to self and to others.

I choose to become curious about the dimensions of me.

I choose to become curious about the dimensions of others in proximity to what I hold to be true in my system.

I choose to use the cube as a vehicle for protection, for honor, for worship, for love, as a holy temple of creation here in the physical dimension where I can meet myself fully, eye to eye with the divine.

I choose to define worship as a celebration of what I hold in my heart.

I choose to live life as continual and ever expanding prayer of heart expansion into higher frequency, utilizing all that ultimately contributes to thriving as a celebration of my life and the potential I was given the opportunity to create with.

I choose to travel.

I choose to know myself as a traveler.

I choose to be in motion.

I choose to know myself as evolution.

I choose to spiral up.

I choose to vibrate at higher octaves and expressions of my pure soul self.

I choose to rotate as a shape, protected.

I choose to know, on a cellular level, what the cube activates inside my body and awareness.

I choose to make use of the shapes in reality that are here to create with me.

I choose integration.

I choose to upgrade.

29- Limitation

I choose to release limitation.

I choose to understand my relationship to limitation.

I choose to accept that there are dimensions of me that operate free of limitation.

I choose to connect to potential.

I choose to understand what potential feels like in my body.

I choose to meet the version of me that knows how to create from freedom.

I choose to live free from limitation.

I choose to become aware of my thought systems.

I choose to become aware of my thoughts systems and the quality of information that moves through my awareness oscillating between limitation and potential.

I choose to filter this information quickly and free of distortion.

I choose to understand what it means in every moment of my daily life to create from choice.

I choose to see the tiny, fractional opportunities in my life as they reveal themselves to me as walking wonders.

I choose the becoming.

I choose to believe life is better than I can imagine.

I choose to become curious about what lives beyond what I can imagine.

I choose to receive the good in all things.

I choose to understand that I alone hold the power to shift my reality in the direction of my choosing.

I choose to connect to my genius.

I choose to understand that innovation does not mean being the first to comprehend a truth in my reality, but rather to be the first to create a solution in my own life.

I choose to understand the depth of that statement.

I choose to engage with the depth of that statement as it unravels itself in my field.

I choose to know what it means to engage with my life field from a position of limitless potential.

I choose to create free of the perceived weight of potential.

I choose to create free of heaviness.

I choose to create free of density.

I choose to understand that possibility is not responsibility.

I choose to take responsibility for creating what is aligned and what interests me in my life.

I choose to accept that nothing can force this responsibility on me.

I choose to understand that I am responsible for what I choose to create.

I choose to know what it feels like in my body to be inspired.

I choose to follow desire.

I choose to remember what desire feels like in my body.

I choose to create from potential.

I choose to create from possibility.

I choose to see myself as capable, innovative, creative, and focused.

30- Templates

I choose to consider the templates.

I choose to observe the templates active in my reality.

I choose to construct, build, and connect to the templates that are here from me, for me, and natural to me to create with.

I choose to see patterns in my life as communicative truth.

I choose to release suffering from the patterns in my life that are speaking to me.

I choose to understand that the patterns that loop in my life, teach me about what is possible for me, when I see and release.

I choose to align to my vision.

I choose to engage in templates as the construction of high level creation that swirls around me, offering me the answers to the questions that I ask.

I choose to ask the right questions.

I choose to live free of self judgment.

I choose to live free of judgment of others.

I choose to have my own experience.

I choose to allow the experience of others to live in parallel proximity.

I choose to learn how to think multidimensionally.

I choose to learn how to think around, under, and through.

I choose to see templates active in my life as multidimensional fields of wisdom.

I choose to see templates active in my life as multidimensional fields of creation.

I choose to translate wisdom into inner knowing that sets me on a path that aligns with my soul blueprint.

I choose to accept that I have a soul blueprint and a human blueprint.

I choose to be the architect of my reality.

I choose to craft a reality deeply seeded in my desire.

I choose to see, engage with, and orient myself to perceive structures of reality that are birthed from my natural desire.

I choose to understand what desire feels like in my body.

I choose to connect to the spark of creation that comes from me.

I choose to connect to an internal drive and alignment with truth in my system at all times.

I choose to accept that I am the architect of my dreams.

I choose to understand the template.

I choose to connect to the blueprint.

I choose to create within the divine frameworks of what is possible in me, for me, and from me.

I choose simple and potent patterns of creation.

I choose to build.

24

THE ROOT SEQUENCE

31-Correction

I choose to free myself in correction.

I choose to become curious about what it means to operate in correct and clean states of personal awareness.

I choose to see the value that correctness can offer me.

I choose to see myself as whole, full, and capable.

I choose to know what correction feels like in my body.

I choose to know what correcting distorted patterns in my life can provide me.

I choose to know what correcting my thought systems can offer me.

I choose to know that I came here with correct and powerful, high frequency potential and organic human intelligence designed to activate me in my dreams and desires.

I choose to engage with the correct aspects of intelligence, internal power, and energy that seeks to serve me in my truth.

I choose to know the difference between healing and correcting.

I choose to know the difference between truth and correction.

I choose to know the difference between shame and my correct nature.

I choose to see the space that is created.

I choose to know what space feels like in my body.

I choose to understand what I value.

I choose to know that there is so much more of me available to me, to be as I am and connect with others in alignment and correct manifestations of my living experience.

I choose to question what is false.

I choose to ask myself what is true.

I choose to know what it feels like to be free of false structures in my body.

I choose to ask myself, is what I am looking at correct in its structural integrity or is there something else here for me to be aware of.

I choose to connect with the answers I receive free of confusion.

I choose to step outside of emotional narratives that are addicted to blaming, shaming, devouring, and self abandonment in order to see myself clearly.

I choose to know what it feels like to be true to myself.

I choose to welcome what comes, in reverence of my own internal state of power.

I choose to live free of powerlessness.

I choose to observe.

I choose to observe the patterns.

I choose to watch how they move.

I choose to see the beginning and the end.

I choose to see the circular motion.

I choose to initiate myself into portals of learning that lead to the correction of self doubt, questioning, and lack of resources in my life field.

I choose to support myself.

I choose to say yes to my soul's frequency.

I choose to know all that is there, all that will be there, and all that was there, in a correct state of awareness and learn to live as it.

I choose to make it simple.

I choose to look at what is.

I choose to release the pressure.

I choose to release self definition connected to getting it right and getting it wrong.

I choose to take responsibility for how I feel about what I choose to create.

I choose to feel myself.

I choose to commit to my truth.

I choose to correct.

32-Perfection

I choose to release my distorted awareness of perfection.

I choose to let go of the ways I allow the concept of perfection to attack or dilute my sense of self.

I choose to understand nature and the universe as perfect.

I choose to see my life as perfect.

I choose to see the opportunities available to me as perfect examples of my ability to create what I dream as a symptom of my aptitude.

I choose coherence.

I choose correctness.

I choose to know the divine motion of alignment as a synchronization and clicking in of my correct and fully expressed essence active in all areas and aspects of my life.

I choose to become curious about what it means to correct myself.

I choose to see myself as correct.

I choose to understand the concept of perfection as an ordered state that the universe moves towards as a mechanism of its inherent nature.

I choose to know that disorder becomes ordered in the vibrations, frequencies, sequences, motions, and behaviors that come into contact with the nature of being.

I choose to know what it feels like in my body to connect to perfection.

I choose to know perfection free of pressure.

I choose to understand that the human definition of perfection is often experienced as a distorted mental framework.

I choose to know that concepts sparked from truth do not equate to truth in an operative manner.

I choose to become corrected in nature.

I choose to become corrected by my higher intelligence.

I choose to become corrected by the way that my system naturally heals itself when I focus on creation.

I choose to know myself as a creation.

I choose to know myself as a full, whole, coherent, mechanically viable, programmable, adept, and joyous system of reality.

I choose to know my inner universe.

I choose to know the motion of my desire.

I choose to know the nature of my elements.

I choose to know the atmosphere of my emotions.

I choose to know the in between state of my dreams in waking moments.

I choose to know myself as a full spectrum operating system.

I choose to accept that I came here with everything that I needed, perfectly aligned to thrive, evolve, and transform.

I choose to walk through the fires of my life with courage in order to return to the fullest expression of myself in the knowing of who I am.

I choose to know myself as perfect.

I choose to move.

33-Wealth

I choose to release lack.

I choose to look at what I value in my life.

I choose to ask myself what it means to be rich.

I choose to release mental definitions and connect to my heart.

I choose to feel the sun on my face.

I choose to hear the rushing frequencies of water.

I choose to rest my feet on the soil.

I choose to feel my heart beating.

I choose to understand that wealth is my birthright.

I choose to know the difference between being wealthy and being rich.

I choose to ask myself what that means to me as an embodied state of being.

I choose to know the divine definition of these states as internal bounty, always growing, always expanding, always available, always responding to my invitation.

I choose to ask myself if what I am experiencing in my life is as full as the richness available to me in every moment.

I choose to take responsibility for the lack that I experience regardless of my personal experience in comparison to others.

I choose to experience what I treasure.

I choose to define what I treasure in my life.

I choose to know that I can treasure myself.

I choose to see myself as valuable.

I choose to understand that investing in my evolution is valuable.

I choose to make moves in my life that align with what I value.

I choose to consider that it is impossible for me to know what is full without me also knowing what is empty.

I choose to consider the perfection in that.

I choose to expand my energy to receive all the good that is encoded in my soul's frequency and attune to the sheer amount of genius and potential that is always, at all times, available to me.

I choose to know that money responds to authority.

I choose to activate a life that exceeds my wildest expectations for what is possible for me, my community, my business, my children, and those around me that I love.

I choose to plant seeds of wealth in my life wherever I go.

I choose to know that money is welcome in my life.

I choose to invite money into my reality in a manner that allows me and others to thrive.

I choose generosity.

I choose to share my love for money, resources, genius, and connection with the world.

I choose to see money as a neutral resource.

I choose to release fear, limitation, cultural programming, collective programming, judgment, pain, and all patterns connected to wealth that keep my system stuck in looping cycles of lack.

I choose to activate new wealth patterns.

I choose to write new narratives about my past, present and future to align to wealth and receiving in my life.

I choose to understand myself as full.

I choose to ask myself what I actually need.

I choose to let go of comparison.

I choose to experience money as easy.

I choose to release any and all power that money has over me.

I choose to activate an internal wealth template that once put in motion gains force in my life, connecting me to all the majestic beauty in the universe and more.

I choose to love my life.

I choose to love the tiny moments.

I choose gratitude.

I choose wealth.

34-Full Spectrum System

I choose to release the idea that I am broken.

I choose to release the concept that I am fragmented.

I choose to release the theory that there are parts of me that I am still searching for.

I choose to release any and all awareness I have defined as truth in my system that I am waiting to fix, heal, or complete an internal reunification process in order to realize myself as whole and correct.

I choose to understand that I am a full spectrum system.

I choose to know the colors of my energy that vibrate on a spectrum of light.

I choose to know that all aspects of me are perfectly designed to create together as one fully operational, coherent, system of creation in order to realize reality as I see fit.

I choose to shift my internal conversations to a state of awareness that acknowledges how what I feel is true instead of false.

I choose to reject the idea of fragmentation.

I choose to reject the idea of compartmentalization.

I choose to reject fragmented truth.

I choose to reject distortion.

I choose to see and experience all facets of my reality as opportunities for me to fully utilize my gifts.

I choose to understand my sensitivity as a state of power.

I choose to know the power of my ego to process data correctly and serve me.

I choose to craft high vibrational emotion.

I choose to connect to essence.

I choose to express myself in inspiration.

I choose to feel joy.

I choose to feel the weight and magnitude of the incredible opportunity I have as a creator to choose how to invest myself and the excitement of what I can do with what I have been gifted.

I choose to see this life as a gift.

I choose to accept my individuality.

I choose to see myself as unique.

I choose to know what it feels like to lead myself forward.

I choose to accept a life of self initiated transformation.

I choose to apply myself in challenging and inspirational ways that align with my capacity as a creator while understanding that if I am bored, it is my responsibility to find what is exciting to me.

I choose to release apathy.

I choose to take responsibility.

I choose to know that I am engaged in creation as a singular matrix separate and connected to the whole.

I choose to understand that everything I engage with in my life operates as a living system.

I choose to know myself as organic, living technology.

I choose to activate my gifts.

I choose to expand into fullness.

I choose to know the technology is within me.

35-Light

I choose to release false light.

I choose to let go of collective light masking itself as expansion in my system.

I choose to let go of collective light masking itself as empowerment in my system.

I choose to let go of collective light masking itself as a choice in my system.

I choose to let go of collective light masking itself as control in my system.

I choose to let go of any and all structures that exist in the light created in the collective from inverted templates in order to gain dominion over my energy.

I choose to release my shadow to the light.

I choose to release my shadow to the dark.

I choose to redefine the concept of shadow in the religious or esoteric teachings of spirituality that would use this to create shame and separation in my system.

I choose to see myself as whole.

I choose to feel in color.

I choose to speak in vibrations.

I choose to hear the multidimensional layers of communication I am immersed in as a living, breathing, expression of the divine.

I choose to expand my essence.

I choose to know what it means to shine.

I choose to define this as a feeling state.

I choose to define this as an embodied state.

I choose to define this as a creative state.

I choose to express myself fully in the potential of what flows from me when I am ignited, joyful, inspired, living from my genius, in action, and fully essenced from my soul's frequency.

I choose the light and the dark.

I choose to find comfort in the in-between.

I choose to experience the gray as a possibility.

I choose to see the magic in my ability to choose.

I choose to take responsibility for the epic nature of my inherent power as a divine expression.

I choose to become the sun.

I choose to know what it means in an active, moving dreamscape for my life to be as easy as being the sun.

I choose to be the center of gravity.

I choose to know how to rest.

I choose to understand that my frequency is my currency.

I choose to know that my energy is my currency.

I choose to apply myself to all aspects of my naturally adept and resilient ability to seed, grow, envision, sustain, and thrive.

I choose to use my light for my benefit.

I choose to release decay.

I choose to compost the energy that I release.

I choose to replace what I release with what is good for the soul.

I choose to know my light.

I choose light.

36-Dark

I choose to release false darkness.

I choose to release darkness that destroys.

I choose to release all darkness that feeds upon the good in my life.

I choose to step into divine nature with the dark and accept myself fully.

I choose to accept myself fully free of addiction.

I choose to accept myself fully while utilizing my higher intelligence to engage in masterful expression of my mind, body, and spirit.

I choose to know the dark as cosmic potential.

I choose to know the dark as a realm of internal peace, genius, vision, and transformation.

I choose to know the truth of chaos in my system.

I choose to know that chaos has nothing to teach me.

I choose to experience the divine balance between light and darkness and take my place as the keeper of a vast and wild landscape of beauty and magic.

I choose to see in the dark.

I choose to enhance my senses in the dark.

I choose to move with the vibrations of creation in this wilderness that is my home.

I choose to weave with the mystery.

I choose to move in flow with what I create in my life.

I choose to embody an active state of regenerative flow that facilitates the deep awakenings of my truth in energy, awareness, and physical manifestation.

I choose to know myself.

I choose to know my genius.

I choose to see with my eyes closed.

I choose to see in crystalline visions.

I choose to hear the tone of clarity as a force of direction.

I choose to feel from this place.

I choose to know, in all moments, the power of my heart in dark spaces, in light spaces, in prismatic spaces that illuminate my dreams from vision to reality.

I choose to awaken.

I choose to dream awake.

I choose to twist the aperture of internal vision to dial into colors, vibrations, and frequencies that are unseen to my human eye.

I choose to see in the dark.

I choose to release fear.

I choose to see what is for me, only for me, in service to what is good for my soul and aligned to my soul's blueprint.

I choose to oscillate.

I choose to stay in motion.

I choose to mold chaos.

I choose to shape my reality.

I choose to become the architect, the artisan, the force and the forge.

I choose to know what it feels like in my body to be the pulse.

I choose to know how to activate this energy in my body.

I choose to understand the definition of the dark as a divine expression.

I choose to engage in practices, methodologies, awarenesses, and systems that

I choose to sit in the presence of wizards.

I choose to never give my energy to places, people, situations, or collective agreements that are devoid of my influence.

I choose to starve what feeds.

I choose to revoke access to my energy in service to thriving.

I choose to know what it feels like in my body to have access to states of hyper-focus that fuel my dreamscape.

I choose to know color.

I choose to know what color feels like in my body.

I choose to touch the fabric of the dark starlight I am made of.

I choose beauty.

I choose myself.

37-Genius X

I choose to know my genius.

I choose to know my genius in this lifetime.

I choose to realize my full potential for art, creativity, innovation, and expression here and now.

I choose to know what it feels like in my body to be fully tapped into the voice of my internal wellspring of potential.

I choose to execute on that potential.

I choose to do whatever it takes to actualize in physical reality the visions and dreams that I deem as meaningful.

I choose to invest in what matters to me.

I choose to see my genius as a worthy investment.

I choose to feel the satisfaction that comes from living from my genius.

I choose to reserve my energy for creation.

I choose to focus on processing data that feeds my ability to create what I dream.

I choose to release what gets in the way of that.

I choose to play in the landscape of leaders and legends.

I choose to look for solutions.

I choose to release sacrifice.

I choose to know what it feels like in my body to have courage.

I choose to develop stamina for what I desire to create in my life, free of overwhelm, victimhood, and slow, dense, or useless movements.

I choose to observe what is useful to me.

I choose to be supported.

I choose to call in and activate the right kind of support in my life that allows me to thrive from my vision.

I choose to speak in a clear and articulated manner about what I am here for and the influence I have on my reality.

I choose to accept that I am never misunderstood by me.

I choose to know what it feels like to understand myself.

I choose to ground myself in the dark cosmic soil of my genius landscape.

I choose to accept that I must craft my journey forward.

I choose to find the souls that are here for me to assist me on my journey.

I choose to surround myself with leaders that offer inspiration.

I choose commitment.

I choose dedication.

I choose to release effort in the direction of activities that life would offer me as a distraction to achieving what is important to me.

I choose to know that when I am in my zone of genius, life is filled with ease.

I choose to know that ease can exist in parallel to effort.

I choose to invest my efforts towards creating with ease.

I choose to tap in.

I choose to plug in.

I choose to be filled with the magic of my natural ability.

I choose my genius.

38-Agency

I choose to know my will.

I choose to know myself as sovereign.

I choose to accept that it is my god given right to influence my reality.

I choose to know my power as a creator.

I choose to release the narratives of powerlessness and programming that I have engaged as the story of my life up until this point of awareness, so that I may take full responsibility for my gifts.

I choose to know when to move.

I choose to know that I am the timeline.

I choose to know that I am the motion.

I choose to remain in motion.

I choose to know what it feels like in my body to move with precision.

I choose to understand that precision comes when I know myself.

I choose to uphold my standards and boundaries as a means of true self preservation.

I choose to know that the more I express myself in my authentic truth, the more the universe responds to me in the truth of who I am.

I choose to know that my truth defines the laws of my reality.

I choose to consider what my truth is.

I choose to take action on truth as a tone of self awareness rather than a collective agreement of societal rules, expectations, projections, designed to distort as a symptom of its programming.

I choose to consider truth free of emotion.

I choose to consider what agency reveals to me when I am free.

I choose to know what agency feels like in my body.

I choose to take responsibility for what I believe in.

I choose to take responsibility for what I engage in.

I choose to take responsibility for what I allow in my life.

I choose to take responsibility for what I allow to exist in my internal system of awareness.

I choose to evolve.

I choose to take steps forward into states of walking wonder.

I choose to surprise myself.

I choose to know what it feels like in my body to be delighted by my clarity and action.

I choose to take action.

I choose to feel how good it feels in my body to take action.

I choose to act.

I choose to release reactive patterns and behavioral habits, that limit my ability to take full responsibility for myself.

I choose to release emotional distortion.

I choose to know that when I truly know myself as a proactive force of motion in reality, there is nothing to fear.

I choose to release control.

I choose to become the flow.

I choose to create in cycles.

I choose to release the pressure of linear timelines and activate new and innovative ways of being with the world in service to my development.

I choose to be an agent of change.

I choose agency.

39-Creativity

I choose to express my creativity.

I choose to know myself as creative.

I choose to release collective definitions of art and comparison as a means to gauge my own ability to create.

I choose to take risks.

I choose to know that I am always supported.

I choose to use creative states as a way of reprogramming myself in the direction of what is good for my soul.

I choose to connect to my essence.

I choose to dance and move my body.

I choose to allow ideas, concepts, inspirations, and art to flow through me as a source of life.

I choose to thrive in my creative essence.

I choose to know what it feels like to move inspiration into action.

I choose to understand that my creative force heals me.

I choose to experience sensation as art.

I choose to experience freedom as art.

I choose to free myself from stifling states of self imposed failure.

I choose to explore art as an immersive dreamscape of creation.

I choose to open my heart.

I choose to speak with confidence.

I choose to try new things.

I choose to have faith.

I choose to take a chance on myself.

I choose to live free from the idea that there is something to lose.

I choose to know that what I can imagine, I can create and express.

I choose to speak about my life in an imaginative way.

I choose to engage in an immersive landscape of color, feeling, emotion, sensation, and sensation as my primary language and connection to my soul.

I choose to engage with myself as a multidimensional landscape of creation.

I choose to imagine what is possible.

I choose to imagine what is more than possible.

I choose to know my potential.

I choose to create.

40-Action

I choose to take action from my full spectrum system.

I choose to take action from the parts of me that are aligned, free of self doubt.

I choose to take action from the parts of myself that I have invested in mastering.

I choose to take action from my future self.

I choose to understand that when I take action, I am creating.

I choose to free myself from the idea that taking action is exhausting.

I choose to free myself from the concept that taking action is a permanent decision I am making about the direction of my future.

I choose to create in cycles.

I choose to let go of expectation and follow my soul's impulse.

I choose to let go of judgment and move in the flow of my life field.

I choose to take action as an empowered, sovereign creator.

I choose to understand that taking action is my natural state of being.

I choose to understand my relationship with time.

I choose to understand that every decision I make and take action on is a step toward wisdom if I operate with correct perception.

I choose to understand that reality is multidimensional and I know when to move and when to sit still.

I choose to find joy in taking action.

I choose to access to regenerative energy that replenishes my system daily.

I choose to keep my Operating System clean and efficient.

I choose to know how to focus on what matters.

I choose to move at the speed of my natural state.

I choose to understand that speed is my natural state.

I choose to move fast and slow at the same time.

I choose to understand that the perception of time lives inside of my awareness.

I choose to know that I am safe when I make big moves in my life.

I choose to understand how to communicate with my life field and converse with the universe.

I choose an accurate perception of reality.

I choose to self lead my operating system.

I choose to communicate with my operating system daily.

I choose to understand how to lead myself forward in the direction of choice and evolution.

I choose to take action daily to create a life filled with wealth and what I value.

I choose to resist hesitation and confusion.

I choose to alchemize the pause.

I choose to engage in forms of creation that transform confusion into clarity.

I choose to know what action to take.

I choose to back myself up.

I choose to know that I am building human skill and learning from my life field.

I choose to know that my life is perfectly orchestrated to unlock layers of deep internal soul wisdom and transformation.

I choose to know that I am always supported.

I choose to know that I am never alone.

I choose to know what it feels like in my body when I am ready to take action.

I choose to move.

DATA SEQUENCE

41-Speed

I choose to move at the speed of my natural state.

I choose to process data with ease.

I choose to allow information to move through my body, mind, and spirit in a way that is conducive with my full spectrum system.

I choose to release whatever gets in the way of that.

I choose to understand that dynamic fields of information are open and morphing, and in that truth, it is my responsibility to organize and manage the data that moves through me.

I choose to release stagnant energy, narrative, information, self doubt, seeking, questioning, and internal lack resource.

I choose to access clean energy.

I choose to access clean data structures.

I choose to know what it feels like in my body to know what is true for me.

I choose to know multidimensional truth.

I choose to know what multidimensional truth feels like in my body.

I choose to release the dissonance.

I choose to release internal conflict.

I choose to connect to my souls ultimate truth and live in service to that as a means of creation and innovation in my life.

I choose to know what it feels like to allow data to move through my body free of consequence.

I choose to know that I am designed to be a conduit for divine intelligence.

I choose to connect to my higher intelligence.

I choose to know what it means to be highly sensitive and self resourced.

I choose to know that I am built to sense and experience complex data fields.

I choose to have a relationship in my body with sensations of truth.

I choose to see clearly.

I choose to release overwhelm.

I choose to support myself in moments of overwhelm through the deep knowing of myself and how to gracefully nurture and maintain an environment that supports me.

I choose to live in a focused and highly creative state that aligns with my genius.

I choose to explore my relationship with time.

I choose to know that time lives in my experience of it.

I choose to know that I can move fast.

I choose to know that I can move slow.

I choose to know that I can expand.

I choose to evolve.

I choose speed.

42-Storage

I choose to manage where I store information, energy, and body experiences.

I choose to consider that my open and highly sensitive state of higher intelligence exists to serve me.

I choose to ask myself, if I am whole, complete, and sovereign, why am I holding onto what I desire to free myself from?

I choose to allow life to provide me with the answers and take the action needed to support myself.

I choose to filter.

I choose to become the yes and the no.

I choose to let energy do the work.

I choose to let it be easy.

I choose to know what it feels like in my body to hold an intention and let my life organize itself around my desire.

I choose to store what I treasure.

I choose to hold my life sacred.

I choose to collect memories that fill me with wonder.

I choose to seek out my truth.

I choose connection.

I choose to fill myself with wealth.

I choose to know what I value.

I choose to connect to the light in my cells and expand into possibility.

I choose to release what limits me.

I choose to release what shrouds my ability to see myself and the world around me clearly.

I choose to release pain.

I choose to release suffering.

I choose to release victimhood.

I choose to consistently release what binds me.

I choose to replace what I release.

I choose to connect to my genius.

I choose to connect to the deep and everlasting wisdom that is here to create with me.

I choose to sink deep into my essence and contemplate how much the narratives from my past are informing my future.

I choose to be the author of my story.

I choose self lead where i store, what I store, the quality of what I store, how I store it, and why.

I choose to know why I do what I do and what it serves.

I choose to store what is good for my soul.

43-Story

I choose to write my own story.

I choose to engage in stories about myself that speak to my power.

I choose to release the stories I hold in my system that deplete my energy.

I choose to understand that the stories I cling to run in the background of my system, draining me of my pure currency and energetic resource.

I choose to understand that stories that free me expand my energy creating a regenerative source of currency that provide me with the fuel to create what I dream.

I choose to carefully craft narratives that speak to my abilities to shift my reality.

I choose to be intentional about how I speak about myself.

I choose to be intentional about how I speak about others.

I choose to be intentional about how I speak about what I can do.

I choose to be careful about how I speak about the learning phases I am in.

I choose to pay attention to how I speak about the architecture of life.

I choose to pay attention to the stories I enroll in.

I choose to know that conversations with others are invitations of energy.

I choose to sit at tables that respect my influence.

I choose to craft a life filled with dreams and magic.

44-Senses

I choose to expand my senses.

I choose to be comfortable with my senses.

I choose to use what I can sense to inform my life in rich and expansive ways.

I choose to release stagnation.

I choose to release what I hold in my body consistently and with intention to be reborn as joy, love, imagination, and magic.

I choose to know what it feels like in my body to be safe with my senses.

I choose to know what it feels like in my body to expand into sensation.

I choose to sense, feel, connect, and interpret what is aligned with the highest expression of my soul's frequency available to me at this moment in the now.

I choose to know what it feels like to connect to the wild and detailed landscape of my inner senses and evolve.

I choose to connect to the subtle energies.

I choose to know what it feels like in my body to connect with the subtle energies of the divine.

I choose to know what it feels like in my body to connect to the subtle energies of my intuition and allow it to inform me to create from my soul's potential.

I choose to be guided.

I choose to be guided by my intuition.

I choose to be guided by the divine.

I choose to be guided by my senses.

I choose to know what it sounds like to connect with my senses.

I choose to know what it looks like for me to visualize with my senses.

I choose to know what it feels like to connect with my senses.

I choose to savor the taste of my senses.

I choose to become the prophecy.

I choose to become the future.

I choose to weave with the past.

I choose to know that I am the consciousness that creates the shift.

I choose to focus on potential.

I choose to create what is good for the soul.

I choose to know that I can manage my sensations.

I choose to hear my truth.

I choose to see my truth.

I choose to feel my truth.

I choose to sense my truth.

I choose to expand into the ever opening and infinite possibilities of my senses they serve me in from my soul's desire.

I choose to know that at any moment, I can care for myself.

I choose to self support.

I choose to know that I am held, safe, loved, protected, perfect, and designed to optimize every gift that I hold in my mind, body, and spirit.

I choose to activate my senses.

45-Security

I choose to know that I am safe.

I choose to feel my yes and my no.

I choose to know that I can protect myself.

I choose to know what it feels like in my body to be protected.

I choose to move through life with an energy of protection that activates my life field with ease and confidence.

I choose to know myself fully.

I choose to know that I am safe being myself.

I choose to know that I am safe expressing myself.

I choose to know that I am safe and free of the judgements of others.

I choose to ask myself, who is the judge of my life?

I choose to know the difference between boundaries that I hold for myself and the way other people behave towards me.

I choose to separate my dependencies within that context to protect my innocent heart.

I choose to release blame.

I choose to release shame.

I choose to step forward into my life knowing that I create my own safety.

I choose to consider what it feels like in my body to be safe in connection to a state of wholeness.

I choose to make peace with my purpose.

I choose to create with the peace in my soul.

I choose to hear the voices of fear that warn me to stay small and guide them back to the truth of my internal architecture.

I choose to connect to the electrical impulse of wholeness.

I choose to connect to the electrical impulse of fullness.

I choose to connect to the electrical impulse of love.

I choose to connect to the electrical impulse of beauty.

I choose to connect to the electrical impulse of wonder.

I choose to connect to the electrical impulse of magic.

I choose to be part of the weaving.

I choose to become the point of creation.

I choose to become the point of destruction.

I choose to see the perfection in challenge as a catalyst for my expansive evolution.

I choose to feel safe in my growth.

I choose to feel safe in my voice.

I choose to hear the tone of safety active in my being as a divine impulse.

I choose to activate balance.

I choose to live deeply in faith.

I choose to know what it means in my life to create with faith as a friend.

I choose to know faith as a guide.

I choose to know that I am always supported.

I choose to know that I will be ok.

I choose to know the divine purpose of chaos and creation.

I choose to trust that I know.

I choose safety.

46-Soul

I choose to connect to my soul.

I choose to know my soul's potential.

I choose to hear the whispers of deep and ancient wisdom calling me forward into the unknown.

I choose to maximize my living experience.

I choose to create what is good for me, I choose to be steeped in my essence.

I choose to create what is good for the world.

I choose to know the full expression of my soul here on earth.

I choose to connect to my life field.

I choose to learn from my life field as the most true and powerful divine teacher, confidant, and companion.

I choose to invest my life, my time, my resources, and my currency to explore the magic that lives within me.

I choose to consider how I can connect more deeply with my soul's magic.

I choose to honor the sacredness within me.

I choose to act with integrity and courage.

I choose to bring my soul's vision into my reality and take purposeful, powerful steps forward in every waking moment of my focus and awareness.

I choose to live in harmony with all creation.

I choose to expand my awareness daily.

I choose to commit to embracing each moment as part of my soul's journey.

I choose to express my authentic essence.

I choose to see beyond my human limitations.

I choose to honor my soul's timing in all things and take action to grow my skills as a creator and a human.

I choose to release fear and live in faith.

I choose to follow the quiet guidance of my inner self.

I choose to know my still power.

I choose to experience my emotions as a bright and colorful prism of soul messages.

I choose to know what it feels like in my body to interpret the messages of my soul in a grounded and pragmatic way that opens my life to a thriving, magical, reality beyond my expectation.

I choose to embody love as the essence of my being.

I choose to nurture my connection with the divine.

I choose to stay present.

I choose to remember my soul's limitless nature and bring light to all parts of myself.

I choose to access wisdom from my higher self and let go of what no longer serves my evolution.

I choose to create a life aligned with my soul's purpose.

I choose to experience myself as a soul human partnership.

I choose to embody my soul's highest potential.

I choose to trust my soul's path, even when it's unknown.

I choose to align my life with my soul's truth.

I choose to live from my soul.

47-Subconscious

I choose to become aware of my subconscious.

I choose to unlock the power of my subconscious mind.

I choose to let my subconscious support my highest good.

I choose to trust the wisdom my subconscious holds and allow my subconscious to serve me effortlessly.

I choose to release limiting beliefs buried in my subconscious.

I choose to intentionally craft empowering thought systems in the corners of my subconscious mind and use them to create states of inner freedom.

I choose to reprogram my subconscious with my intentions.

I choose to feel safe accessing the depths of my subconscious and allow my subconscious to support my goals.

I choose to reframe past experiences stored in my subconscious.

I choose to clear fears rooted in my subconscious mind and expand into the limitless aspects of my focus.

I choose to create peace in my subconscious mind.

I choose to align my subconscious with my conscious intentions.

I choose to heal subconscious patterns that no longer serve me.

I choose to believe in my unlimited potential.

I choose to bring my subconscious into harmony with my desires.

I choose to rewire old patterns for freedom and growth and replace self-doubt with unwavering confidence.

I choose to allow my subconscious to open new pathways for success.

I choose to cultivate beliefs that support my evolution.

I choose to let go of old fears that keep me from thriving while I remain committed to reframing my subconscious associations with wealth and abundance.

I choose to connect to my subconscious and alchemize challenges as a reservoir of creativity.

I choose to access the hidden wisdom in my subconscious mind.

I choose to see myself as whole and complete.

I choose to trust in the healing abilities of my subconscious and feel at ease exploring my inner world.

I choose to clear subconscious blocks around success and replace old stories with new, empowering truths.

I choose to forgive and release past experiences stored inside of my mind, body, and spirit.

I choose to harmonize my subconscious beliefs with my dreams.

I choose to connect with my subconscious to create with ease.

I choose to align my subconscious with my highest purpose.

I choose to be present.

I choose to remain lucid.

I choose to be awake.

I choose my will.

I choose to focus.

48-Systems

I choose to know my systems.

I choose to create systems that align with the way I work as an individual expression and accept myself fully in that pursuit.

I choose to know where to organize data in my system.

I choose to create systems that support my growth.

I choose to build systems that enhance my efficiency.

I choose to align my systems with my highest goals.

I choose to release systems that no longer serve me and streamline my creations for ease and clarity.

I choose integration.

I choose to design systems that align with my soul's truth and the unique wiring I hold to operate at optimum output.

I choose simplification.

I choose to simplify my systems to reduce overwhelm.

I choose to trust in what I create.

I choose to be consistent in consistency, allowing my full spectrum system to flourish within the boundaries of my divine will.

I choose to know what it feels like in my body to be devoted.

I choose to support my evolution.

I choose to release outdated habits, patterns, and sequences from my life field that limit me.

I choose adaptable systems

I choose dynamic growth.

I choose to let go of rigid systems that limit me.

I choose to create systems that inspire and energize me.

I choose to build systems that allow for flexibility.

I choose to know what it feels like in my body to trust the orbits I create and connect to the spherical wisdom of life.

I choose to upgrade my systems as I grow.

I choose to create systems that bring joy into my routine.

I choose to use systems to support my financial freedom.

I choose to optimize systems that strengthen my relationships.

I choose to create systems that maximize my strengths.

I choose to set up systems that support long-term success and organize my environment for ease and focus.

I choose to integrate systems that align with my energy, integrity, and internal states of support.

I choose physical wellness.

I choose mental clarity.

I choose resilience.

I choose optimal flow.

I choose evolution.

I choose self-respect.

I choose to align my systems with my spiritual journey.

I choose to embody efficiency in all my systems.

I choose to continuously improve my systems for simplicity.

I choose to let my systems guide me free of confinement.

I choose to trust my intuition to assist me in creating effective systems that infuse my life with purpose and meaning.

I choose to establish systems that empower my creativity.

I choose to honor the process of building sustainable systems.

I choose to thrive.

49-Seventh Sense

I choose to trust my seventh sense fully.

I choose to cultivate awareness of my seventh sense.

I choose to be open to higher guidance in all moments.

I choose to feel the presence of my higher awareness.

I choose to know what this presence feels like in my body.

I choose to perceive beyond the ordinary.

I choose to live beyond the ordinary.

I choose to reach for the stars.

I choose to sense the constellations and weavings of the fabric of life that surrounds me.

I choose to recognize the subtle energies around me.

I choose to integrate my seventh sense into daily life.

I choose to respect the insights my seventh sense brings.

I choose to ask myself: what can I perceive when I activate all aspects of higher frequencies and sensation available to me?

I choose to strengthen my connection to my higher self.

I choose to embrace wisdom beyond logic.

I choose my inner vision and perception.

I choose to trust what my seventh sense reveals to me.

I choose to feel the flow of my inner guidance.

I choose to explore the depth of my inner awareness.

I choose to honor the insights from my seventh sense.

I choose to develop clarity in higher perception.

I choose to stay grounded while accessing my higher knowing.

I choose to act with confidence in my intuitive knowing.

I choose to listen deeply to the voice within.

I choose to align with the truth my seventh sense shows me.

I choose to experience the fullness of my perceptive abilities.

I choose to connect to the greater intelligence within me, that surrounds me, that is part of me, and that is part of the whole.

I choose to welcome profound understanding into my life.

I choose to observe the subtle energies that guide me.

I choose to engage fully with my higher awareness.

I choose to receive insights from beyond the physical senses.

I choose to strengthen my bond with universal wisdom.

I choose to elevate my awareness to a higher plane and remain receptive to the messages of my soul.

I choose to integrate the wisdom of my seventh sense.

I choose to trust in the power of unseen truths.

I choose to enhance my ability to perceive energy.

I choose to be curious about the depths of my perception.

I choose to transcend surface understanding and embrace the mystery of my seventh sense.

I choose to discern the guidance from my higher self.

I choose to feel safe in exploring expanded awareness.

I choose to know what this safety feels like in my body.

I choose to honor the language of my seventh sense and speak to my life field.

I choose to trust the timing of my higher knowing.

I choose to grow in confidence as I expand my awareness while navigating my life field through the higher dimensions of alchemy.

I choose to experience non dual states of vibration.

I choose to embody the truth that my seventh sense reveals.

I choose to receive information from realms beyond thought.

I choose to receive information from realms beyond limitation.

I choose to receive information from realms beyond imagination.

I choose to receive information from realms beyond what I can perceive at any moment, aligning with the true genius of the divine available to me as my birthright.

I choose to ground my higher awareness in daily habits, actions, perceptions, and perspectives.

I choose to be open to spiritual insights without fear.

I choose to know that I am safe.

I choose to refine my ability to sense the unseen.

I choose to expand my consciousness with every experience.

I choose to feel fully connected to my seventh sense.

I choose the seventh sense.

50-Sphere

I choose to stand upon my reality.

I choose to enter the sphere of limitless potential.

I choose to embrace the wholeness within the sphere.

I choose to connect with the boundless energy of the sphere.

I choose to align myself with the infinite nature of the sphere.

I choose to perceive from a spherical, multidimensional perspective.

I choose to see all experiences as part of my inner sphere.

I choose to know my singular matrix.

I choose to see myself as separate from the whole.

I choose to know myself as whole.

I choose to integrate all aspects of myself within the sphere.

I choose to access all realms within the unity of the sphere and expand into the vastness of my inner realms while I learn to ask better questions of my life field.

I choose to trust in the safety of the spherical field around me.

I choose to recognize the unity and oneness within the sphere.

I choose to align with the pure energy of the spherical field.

I choose to move in harmony with the energy of the sphere.

I choose to feel complete and whole within the sphere.

I choose to access deeper knowledge from within the sphere.

I choose to release any limits within my personal sphere.

I choose to embody the expansive consciousness of the sphere.

I choose to feel centered within the wholeness of the sphere.

I choose to access all perspectives within the sphere.

I choose to resonate with the timeless energy of the sphere.

I choose to honor the wisdom that flows through the sphere.

I choose to align my life with the integrity of the sphere.

I choose to experience the multidimensional nature of the sphere.

I choose to navigate all directions from within my sphere.

I choose to become the north.

I choose to become the south.

I choose to become the west.

I choose to become the east.

I choose to become the up.

I choose to become the down.

I choose to become the center.

I choose to know my spherical awareness.

I choose to expand my perspective to know the infinite nature of the sphere.

I choose to experience oneness in the flow of the sphere.

I choose to find balance and stillness within the sphere.

I choose to feel grounded within the boundless sphere.

I choose to embody the harmony of the spherical field.

I choose to honor my sacred connection to the sphere.

I choose to experience peace within the infinite sphere.

I choose to explore the vast potential held in the sphere.

I choose to let go of resistance within the sphere's energy.

I choose to feel the eternal nature of the sphere within me.

I choose to embrace all experiences as facets of my sphere.

I choose to release fear within the protective field of the sphere.

I choose to know myself as the center of my own sphere.

I choose to embody infinite love within the sphere of being.

I choose to expand my awareness within the spherical dimension.

I choose to trust in the natural balance of the sphere.

I choose to activate my potential from within the sphere.

I choose to experience my consciousness as spherical wholeness.

I choose to create my reality from the unity of the sphere.

I choose to stand upon the sphere.

THE FUTURE OF THE NEW EGO THEORY IN DIVINEOS

The New Ego Theory has already redefined how we think about the ego, offering a powerful tool for personal and spiritual growth. But this is just the beginning. As we look toward the future, the potential applications of this theory extend far beyond individual transformation. The New Ego Theory, within the DivineOS framework, could influence collective human evolution, shaping how we approach everything from mental health to societal progress.

In this chapter, we'll explore the future possibilities for this theory and how it may evolve in conjunction with advances in psychology, neuroscience, technology, and spirituality. We'll also consider the ethical and philosophical implications of consciously reprogramming the ego, especially as more people begin to understand the power they hold in shaping their inner and outer worlds.

Evolving Beyond Current Human Limits: The Expanding Role of The New Ego Theory

As human beings, we are constantly evolving—physically, mentally, and spiritually. The New Ego Theory presents a framework that empowers individuals to accelerate this evolution by consciously reprogramming their ego to align with their highest potential. But what happens when this process becomes widespread? What would it look like for humanity if we collectively embraced the ego as a tool for intentional evolution?

- Future Applications in Personal Development: As more people adopt the principles of The New Ego Theory, we can expect to see significant shifts in how individuals approach personal development. Imagine a world where people are no longer trapped in the cycles of self-doubt, fear, or limiting beliefs. Instead, they use choice commands and intentional programming to move through challenges with clarity and confidence. The ego, once seen as an obstacle, becomes a tool for continuous growth.

- Social and Cultural Shifts: On a societal level, The New Ego Theory has the potential to influence collective behaviors. As more people consciously reprogram their ego, social systems and cultural norms could evolve to prioritize empowerment, collaboration, and authenticity. In a world where individuals are aligned with their divine potential, competition could give way to cooperation, and fear-based decisions could be replaced with love-based, growth-oriented choices.

- Example: Consider the potential impact in education. If schools began teaching children how to use choice commands to reprogram their ego, future generations would grow up understanding that they have control over their internal narratives. Instead of being conditioned by fear of failure or societal pressure, children would learn to process challenges as opportunities for growth and development.

Technological Integration: Ego Reprogramming in the Age of AI and Neuroscience

The future of The New Ego Theory also intersects with the rapid advancements we're seeing in technology and neuroscience. As we gain more understanding of how the brain processes information and how technology can be used to enhance mental and emotional well-being, The New Ego Theory could become a key player in the evolution of human consciousness.

- AI and Personalized Ego Coaching: One potential development is the integration of artificial intelligence with The New Ego Theory. Imagine AI-driven personal assistants designed to help individuals manage their ego's processing systems in real time. These assistants could analyze your emotional state, identify limiting beliefs, and offer personalized choice commands to help you reprogram your internal narrative in the moment.

  ◦ Example: An AI-powered app could track your thought patterns throughout the day and offer reminders like, "You're feeling anxious about this presentation. I recommend using the choice command: 'I choose to trust my preparation and present with confidence.'" This integration of technology would make the process of ego reprogramming even more accessible and practical in everyday life.

- Neuroscience and Brain Mapping: Advances in neuroscience and brain mapping could also deepen our understanding of how choice commands and ego reprogramming work on a neurological level. As we learn more about neuroplasticity and how the brain can be rewired through intentional programming, we could develop more targeted techniques for ego reprogramming that enhance specific areas of personal development.

  ◦ Example: Future research might identify specific neural pathways associated with self-doubt or fear of failure. With this knowledge, practitioners of The New Ego Theory could develop even more precise choice commands that directly target and rewire these neural circuits, creating faster and more effective transformation.

Ethical and Philosophical Considerations: The Responsibility of Conscious Ego Reprogramming

As with any powerful tool, the ability to consciously reprogram the ego comes with significant ethical and philosophical considerations. The New Ego Theory provides individuals with the tools to shape their internal reality, but this power also raises important questions about the nature of free will, self-determination, and the potential risks of misuse.

- Free Will and Autonomy: One of the core philosophical questions surrounding The New Ego Theory is the issue of free will. If we have the ability to reprogram our ego to align with a specific narrative or outcome, how does this affect our sense of autonomy? Are we truly making free choices, or are we simply creating new patterns that guide us in predetermined ways?

  ◦ Response: The New Ego Theory enhances free will by giving individuals the ability to consciously choose their internal programming. Rather than being driven by unconscious conditioning or external influences, people who practice ego reprogramming are actively participating in their own growth and evolution. This theory empowers individuals to take control of their own minds and direct their lives with intention.

- The Risk of Manipulation: Another ethical consideration is the potential for misuse of ego reprogramming techniques. As more people become aware of the power of intentional programming, there's a risk that these tools could be used to manipulate others for personal or societal gain.

  ◦ Response: To mitigate this risk, it's essential to promote the use of The New Ego Theory within a framework of integrity and ethical responsibility. Practitioners must be guided by principles of respect, empowerment, and authenticity, ensuring that ego reprogramming is used to uplift and align individuals with their higher purpose, rather than to control or exploit.

- Philosophical Implications for Self-Identity: Finally, we must consider the philosophical implications of consciously reprogramming the ego in relation to self-identity. If we have the ability to constantly update our internal narrative, how do we maintain a sense of stable identity? Is the ego meant to be a static representation of who we are, or is it naturally fluid and adaptable?

  ○ Response: The New Ego Theory suggests that the ego is inherently fluid and designed for adaptability. Rather than clinging to a fixed sense of self, individuals who embrace this theory understand that identity is a dynamic process. By aligning the ego with divine potential, we create a stable foundation for growth, even as the specifics of our internal narrative evolve over time.

The Collective Evolution of Consciousness

The New Ego Theory also has the potential to influence collective human consciousness. As more individuals reprogram their ego to align with their highest potential, we will see shifts not only on an individual level but also on a societal and global scale. This theory could become a catalyst for a new wave of human evolution, one in which we collectively embrace our ability to shape our internal and external realities.

- Collective Reprogramming: Imagine a world where entire communities practice ego reprogramming, consciously aligning their narratives with empowerment, compassion, and growth. This collective shift could lead to the transformation of social systems, politics, and cultural norms, as individuals move beyond fear-based thinking and into a state of collaborative evolution.

- Spiritual Integration: The New Ego Theory could also deepen our spiritual connection as a collective. By aligning the ego with divine potential, individuals may feel more connected to each other and to the larger universe, fostering a sense of unity consciousness. This could pave the way for global movements toward peace, sustainability, and collective well-being.

• Example: In the future, spiritual communities might integrate The New Ego Theory into their practices, teaching individuals how to reprogram their ego as part of their spiritual development. This could lead to a more enlightened society, where personal growth and collective evolution go hand in hand.

The Ego as a Catalyst for Evolution

At its core, The New Ego Theory is about transformation. But this transformation extends beyond the individual—it has the potential to shape humanity's collective evolution. When we consciously align our ego with divine potential, we open the door to a new era of spiritual awakening and personal empowerment.

• Bridging the Divine and the Human: The ego, in its role as a data processor, serves as the bridge between divine energy and human action. It is the translator of divine intention into tangible results. When aligned with our higher consciousness, the ego becomes the vehicle through which our divine potential is expressed in the physical world.

◦ Example: Think of the ego as a lens. When it is clouded by fear, doubt, and limiting beliefs, our divine light is obscured, and our actions are misaligned with our true purpose. But when the ego is reprogrammed and clarified through intentional choice, that lens becomes clear, allowing divine light to shine through, guiding our actions with precision and purpose.

• Accelerating Collective Evolution: The ripple effect of individual transformation cannot be understated. As more people begin to apply the principles of The New Ego Theory, we will see a shift in collective consciousness. The ego, once viewed as a source of separation, becomes a tool for unity, collaboration, and collective growth.

- Example: When individuals reprogram their ego to align with compassion, abundance, and empowerment, those shifts are reflected in their interactions with others. Imagine a world where communities consciously practice ego reprogramming, fostering environments of collaboration, creativity, and love. The result is a collective awakening, where the ego no longer divides but unites us in our shared pursuit of spiritual and personal evolution.

The future of The New Ego Theory holds incredible promise for both individual and collective evolution. As technology and neuroscience advance, we will develop even more effective ways to reprogram the ego, deepening our understanding of how intentional programming shapes our lives. However, with this power comes great responsibility. The ethical and philosophical implications of conscious ego reprogramming require careful consideration as we move into a future where the lines between psychology, spirituality, and technology continue to blur.

As we look ahead, one thing is certain: The New Ego Theory will play a pivotal role in helping humanity unlock its divine potential, evolve beyond current limitations, and create a more empowered, connected world.

Take the Next Step with Me

You've begun transforming your reality with *The New Ego Theory*. Ready to go further? Join the Guild for community support, explore personalized mentorship, or participate in workshops tailored to your growth.

Visit the links below to choose your path forward today!

The Sinatia Guild. Rebel, Create, Lead - **sinatia.com/guild**

Work with us in 1:1 Mentorship - **sinatia.com/mentorship**

Get the Soul Potential CEO Newsletter - **sinatia.com/newsletter**

CITED STUDIES

Empirical Studies and Theoretical Frameworks
1. Cognitive Load Theory (CLT)
- **Primary Reference:** Sweller, J. (1988). "Cognitive Load During Problem Solving: Effects on Learning." Cognitive Science.
  - **Summary:** Sweller's research introduced Cognitive Load Theory, which argues that learning is more effective when the instructional design does not overload the learner's cognitive capacity. The theory differentiates between intrinsic, extraneous, and germane cognitive loads, suggesting that reducing extraneous load can significantly enhance learning efficiency.

  https://mrbartonmaths.com/resourcesnew/8.%20Research/Explicit%20Instruction/Cognitive%20Load%20during%20problem%20solving.pdf

2. Decision Fatigue
- **Primary Reference:** Vohs, K. D., Baumeister, R. F., et al. (2008). "Making Choices Impairs Subsequent Self-Control: A Limited-Resource Account of Decision Making, Self-Regulation, and Active Initiative." Journal of Personality and Social Psychology.
  - **Summary:** This study demonstrates that making repeated decisions reduces the ability to make further decisions, a phenomenon known as decision fatigue. Simplifying decision-making processes can help maintain cognitive resources and improve decision quality over time.

  https://www.ncbi.nlm.nih.gov/pmc/articles/PMC6119549/

3. The Paradox of Choice
- **Primary Reference:** Schwartz, B. (2004). "The Paradox of Choice: Why More is Less."
  - **Summary:** Barry Schwartz argues that eliminating consumer choices can greatly reduce anxiety for shoppers. Excessive choices can lead to decision paralysis and dissatisfaction, suggesting that simplification can lead to better mental health and decision outcomes.

  https://en.wikipedia.org/wiki/The_Paradox_of_Choice

4. Effects of Mindfulness on Cognitive Simplicity
- **Primary Reference:** Zeidan, F., Johnson, S. K., et al. (2010). "Mindfulness Meditation Improves Cognition: Evidence of Brief Mental Training." Consciousness and Cognition.
  - **Summary:** This study found that brief mindfulness meditation training significantly improved cognitive control, working memory, and executive functioning, indicating

that practices which promote a present-focused, simplified mindset can enhance mental performance.

https://www.sciencedirect.com/science/article/abs/pii/S1053810010000681

5. Psychological Complexity and Well-Being
- **Primary Reference:** Lyubomirsky, S., Sheldon, K. M., et al. (2005). "Pursuing Happiness: The Architecture of Sustainable Change." Review of General Psychology.
  - **Summary:** This review discusses how managing psychological complexity through intentional activities and simplified goal-setting can lead to sustained happiness and well-being.

https://www.ncbi.nlm.nih.gov/pmc/articles/PMC4380267/

ABOUT THE AUTHOR

Tia Marie, visionary founder of The Sinatia Guild, merges pragmatic insight with spiritual depth to empower creators and seekers worldwide. With a legacy spanning multi-million dollar ventures, Tia redefines personal mastery and spiritual expansion through her pioneering methodology. Her work, centered on the essence of the Soul, delves into the energetic structures that shape reality, guiding clients to align with their innate power and potential. Known for her revolutionary approaches to manifestation, soul mentorship, and self-realization, Tia crafts programs that inspire clients to shatter limitations, harness untapped potential, and embody purposeful transformation. *The New Ego Theory* brings her unique insights to the forefront, offering readers a pathway to elevate their consciousness and embody their highest potential through a transformative, soul-driven framework.

https://www.sinatia.com/links

www.ingramcontent.com/pod-product-compliance
Lightning Source LLC
Chambersburg PA
CBHW030635110125
20180CB00045B/743